HAA 230D

FERRARI

FERRARI

THE LEGEND ON THE ROAD

Brian Laban

CHARTWELL
BOOKS, INC.

This edition published 2000 by
Chartwell Books, Inc.
A division of Book Sales, Inc.
114 Northfield Avenue,
Edison, New Jersey 08837
USA

© Chrysalis Books 2000

ISBN 0-7858-1222-9

ACKNOWLEDGEMENTS
The editor is most grateful to the Ferrari owners who so
willingly allowed their cars to be photographed for this book.
Special thanks go to Lord Brocket, whose superb collection at
Brocket Hall forms the backbone of this book; also to Steve Gwyther
at Brocket Hall for his expertise and patience in all weathers. Terry Hoyle
gave time, advice and permission to photograph Ferraris in his keeping in
the early days of the book; Maranello Concessionaires were, as ever, most
helpful. Ferrari photographs on pages 160–75 courtesy of Ferrari UK.
All other Ferraris in this book except the F40 and Testarossa, which
were photographed in Italy courtesy of Ferrari, are in private ownership
in the United Kingdom. Fiat Corporate Communications gave
permission to use early archive photographs in the Introduction.

Production by Omnipress, Eastbourne
Printed in Italy

CONTENTS

INTRODUCTION

In December 1946, *Autocar* opened their announcement of a 'New Italian Make' with the comment 'Not even war damage and the threat of Communism have yet stopped Italian enthusiasm for cars of the supersports type'. They went on to outline 'an entirely new make, the Ferrari 125, which is to be built at a modern works at Maranello . . . ' They then revealed plans for three models built on similar chassis, and called sports, competition and Grand Prix respectively.

On the basis of announced specifications and without ever having seen a car, they gave the marque an enthusiastic welcome. They already knew Enzo Ferrari well of course, but as a team manager with Alfa Romeo, not yet as a manufacturer in his own right; nevertheless, they expected the new Ferrari car to appear for the first time in sports car racing sometime in 1947.

From the outset, the tone of everything written about the new marque indicated a high level of respect for the people involved, and a flattering anticipation of successes to come. Even so, it seems highly unlikely that anyone, even the greatest optimist, could yet have envisaged just what Ferrari would grow into.

Or anyone, perhaps, other than Ferrari himself.

Ferrari was a fast developer and almost frighteningly single-minded. Within a matter of months the motoring press were reporting race wins for the cars from Maranello and within a couple of years it was almost as though Ferrari as a make had been on the racing and sporting car scene forever.

Ferrari wasn't an engineer. He was born in February 1898 in Modena, the son of a metalworker who ran his own modest but prosperous business. While his older brother Alfredo pleased his father by studying engineering, Enzo toyed with ambitions of being a journalist, specifically a sports journalist, or perhaps even an opera singer, but he hated formal studying.

Type 815, 1940, designed by Carrozzeria Touring.

Enzo Ferrari in 1920, driving in his second Targa Florio.

Then in September 1908 his father took him to nearby Bologna to see Felice Nazzaro's Fiat winning the Coppa Florio road race, and from that moment the ten-year-old Ferrari knew exactly where his career would be.

It wouldn't be an easy option. His father and brother died within a few months of each other in 1916 and in 1917. Enzo was conscripted into the army, which was, of course, deeply engaged in World War 1. He served first as a blacksmith with the artillery but he was constantly dogged by ill-health and spent much of his service career in and out of hospitals until he was discharged in 1918, with no desire to rekindle the family business, just that long-term ambition to be a racing driver.

The letter of introduction from the army failed to win him a job with Fiat, but he did find work with a Torinese engineer who was rebuilding redundant light military vehicles to satisfy the small civilian market. Ferrari used to drive the vehicles mainly between Turin and Milan where they were rebodied, and in doing so he made the contact who brought his ambitions nearer.

That was Ugo Sivocci, a racing driver and test driver for CMN, a Milanese company which was also converting ex-military vehicles but which had sporting ambitions well beyond that. Sivocci introduced Ferrari to CMN and Ferrari became another test driver. In October 1919 that gave him his first taste of competition, when he finished fourth in his class in the Parma Poggio di Berceta hillclimb. In November, Ferrari and Sivocci competed with improved CMNs in the 1919 Targa Florio. Both drove their cars down to Sicily, and Ferrari reportedly survived an attack by a pack of wolves in the wintry mountains because he had a small revolver amongst his kit . . . In the race he finished ninth, with Sivocci seventh, but many hours behind the winner.

CMN itself lasted only until 1923, but Ferrari and Sivocci

Ferrari type 125 in its racing debut at Piacenza, 11 May 1947, Franco Cortese at the wheel.

Battista 'Pinin' Farina and Enzo Ferrari.

both left in 1920 and both joined Alfa, a company which already had a fine racing reputation. Enzo finished second for his new employers in the 1920 Targa Florio (behind illustrious team-mate Giuseppe Campari), but his racing career never had any great impact. He scored his share of minor successes but he was always prone to the ill-health that had punctuated his brief military career, and it seems that he was aware too of his own limitations. In 1924, for instance, he should have driven one of the four works Alfa P2s in the Lyons Grand Prix, but missed the race through what seems to have been a nervous breakdown. Some see it as an attack of common sense about his real abilities as a top-level racing driver, brought home perhaps by the death of his long-time friend Sivocci in a practice accident at the 1923 Italian Grand Prix.

Either way, Ferrari was moving more and more towards a role as an organiser. He finally retired as a driver, and probably with a degree of relief, in January 1932, on the birth of his son Dino; by then he had laid the foundations for a much longer term career as a team manager.

From his early days at Alfa he had scouted for new engineering and design talent, attracting to the company such people as Luigi Bazzi and Vittorio Jano, two of the finest automobile engineers and designers in the business, and incidentally both from previously pre-eminent Fiat. In 1929 though, Ferrari was given the opportunity to go it alone, setting up Scuderia Ferrari under the prancing horse banner to run Alfa cars on behalf of some of the wealthier contacts he had made while racing with the factory team. When Alfa themselves began to suffer increasingly severe financial problems in the mid-1930s, Scuderia Ferrari effectively became the works racing team, indirectly supported by the government funds that were keeping the company alive.

The old – Ferrari type 125 at the Maranello factory.

And the new – the sublime F40.

Under Ferrari's management, it became one of the most successful teams on the Grands Prix circuits until the Nazi-backed Mercedes and Auto-Union onslaught just before World War 2.

In 1938 when Alfa reformed an official works team, Ferrari – now a major figure in European racing – went back to manage it, but the return was short-lived. Ferrari had never been particularly tolerant of those he didn't respect and having tasted the freedom and power of running his own organisation he was clearly frustrated by some of the people he had to work with back in Alfa Corse, such as the Spanish engineer Wilfredo Ricart, who seems to have been a fair match for Ferrari in terms of arrogance.

Within a year, the clashes of personality had come to a head and Ferrari left Alfa with a financial settlement and a small group of colleagues (notably including Bazzi), but also an agreement that he wouldn't go racing again under his own name and in direct competition with Alfa for four years. He set up an engineering and design consultancy under the name of Auto Avio Costruzione, in Modena, but if he had intended to stick to the letter of his agreement with Alfa, his intentions didn't last.

In 1940, Ferrari produced two small sports cars, Fiat-based, with eight-cylinder engines of just 1½ litres, and entered them in the Mille Miglia. The cars didn't bear the Ferrari name but were simply called 815s, for the number of cylinders and their capacity. Both led their class before retiring, and if Alfa had been inclined to complain, more important events overtook the world before they had the chance.

By the time World War 2 ended in 1945, Ferrari's obligation to Alfa had expired but his ambition had faded not one bit. The press announcements of late 1946 marked the start of his career as a manufacturer under his own name; the cars in this book tell one side of the Ferrari story from there on.

166MM
BARCHETTA

Maranello is a medium-sized town in the Emilia Romagna region of central northern Italy, around ten miles due south of Modena where Enzo Ferrari was born, and some 20 miles west of Bologna, the region's capital. It is the home of Ferrari cars.

Ferrari moved Auto Avio Costruzione there from Modena in 1943, in the limbo years of World War 2, between his final severance from Alfa Romeo and his emergence as a car maker under his own name. Through the war years, Auto Avio was a substantial company, employing more than 100 workers, building small aero engines and other military mechanical equipment. The works were bombed late in 1944 and again early in 1945, but Ferrari managed to survive, and all through the war he was planning an early re-emergence from the frustration of being a military hardware maker to the joys of being a racing car constructor. And because his obligations to Alfa would by then have expired, that meant he could be a racing car constructor under his own name.

Astonishingly soon after the war ended, with Italy defeated, broke and in political turmoil, Ferrari announced his intention to build Grand Prix cars, competition sports cars, and sports cars for the road – the last named to help finance the first two. Coming from many people that would have sounded like absurdly optimistic posturing, but those reporters who knew Ferrari conveyed no hint of doubt that the cars would come to fruition.

He had about him Luigi Bazzi as chief engineer, and Gioacchino Colombo (the genius who had designed the all-conquering Alfa 158) as engine designer. Both had been with Ferrari in the Alfa racing days, Bazzi almost continuously since the early 1920s, Colombo renewing his links in 1946.

While much larger companies recovered slowly from the war, Ferrari blazed onto the scene with the audaciously complex and advanced 125 family of cars. All were based around a brand-new engine designed by Colombo. It displaced a modest 1½ litres, but in the extraordinarily ambitious shape of a short-stroke V12, with a single overhead camshaft to each cylinder bank and racing

In a run of less than fifty 166MMs, about half were the classic *barchetta* by Touring (below) and all of those were in the first series. Detail design varied from car to car, but the little boat, on its Borrani wheels (opposite), was kept simple.

In the late 1940s, the one-piece styling of the *barchetta* (overleaf) was way ahead of most of its cycle-winged contemporaries.

motorcyle-type hairpin valve springs to allow outstandingly compact heads. Ferrari's love of the classic V12 configuration reportedly began when he saw pictures of an early Packard V12 and continued virtually through his life.

The 125s duly appeared early in 1947. Within months they had started to win races. Only two were built, one with a cycle-winged body, the other with a rather prettier full-width shell, by Touring of Milan. Ferrari was a manufacturer now, but still a very small one.

He didn't intend that to last for long. Good as Colombo's tiny jewel of an engine was (with up to 118bhp claimed in its unsupercharged competition form) it was only the beginning and, with a new Formula 2 category for unsupercharged cars of up to 2 litres now proposed, Ferrari's next move was fairly predictable.

The first increase in capacity came late in 1947 with the 1.9-litre 159, which Bazzi contrived by increasing both the bore and the stroke. As with the 125, only two 159s were built, one of them apparently converted from the original 125C. A 159 won the Turin Grand Prix in October 1947, but the interim model was quickly superseded by a full 2-litre model, the first 166.

This stretching of the 'short-block' Colombo V12 took two more stages, first via a further bore increase, to 1992cc; then, after just a few examples of that engine, by another

tiny stroke increase, to 1995cc. The 166 naturally stood for the capacity of one cylinder, in the way of all Ferrari type numbering in the very early days.

The series was announced in November 1947, and by 1948 it was frequently described as 'the most advanced unsupercharged sports car in the world today'. It appeared in several variants. The first was the Spyder Corsa, a cycle-winged car with tacked-on headlight pods. It looked a little unsure as to whether it was a single-seater or a two-seater, but in a way it served as both, equally usable in either sports car racing or the new Formula 2 events. With three Weber carburettors, the Spyder Corsa claimed as much as 150bhp. The 166 Sport was a touring version of the same theme, with around 90bhp, but only a couple were built, a spyder and a coupé, both bodied by Allemano.

And then came the beautiful 166MM. It was launched in November 1948, at the Turin Show, the first show where Ferrari had exhibited and where he also chose to unveil the 166 Inter. The Inter was presented as a Touring-bodied coupé, which was effectively Ferrari's first real road car which could go racing too. The MM was subtly different; as with previous Ferraris, it was principally intended for racing, but maybe more than any other Ferrari racer to date it was viable as a road car too. Ferrari even offered competition and 'touring' versions, mainly distinguished

Although the 166MM was a first step towards series production, it was also a racer. Its cockpit (above left) was functional but hardly luxurious, the three-carb Colombo engine (left) had grown, and luggage space (above) was not a priority.

Superleggera construction was already strong, but touches like the sweeps on the nose (above left) added stiffness as well as style to light panels, while the hood scoop (left) and plain, comprehensive instruments were strictly functional.

**166MM BARCHETTA
SPECIFICATION**

ENGINE
60° V12

CAPACITY
1995cc

BORE x STROKE
60.0 × 58.8mm

COMPRESSION RATIO
10.0:1

POWER
140bhp

VALVE GEAR
Single overhead camshafts

FUEL SYSTEM
Three Weber 32DCF carburettors

TRANSMISSION
Five-speed manual

FRONT SUSPENSION
Independent, by double wishbones, transverse leaf spring, lever dampers

REAR SUSPENSION
Non-independent, by live axle, semi-elliptic leaf springs, parallel arms, lever dampers

BRAKES
All drums

WHEELS
Centre-lock wire

WEIGHT
c.1430lb (648kg)

MAXIMUM SPEED
c.135mph (217kph)

NUMBER MADE, DATES
c.46, 1948–53

by their cockpit trim. The changes weren't concessions exactly, something more like a broadening of mind.

The MM stood for Mille Miglia, to capitalise on Clemente Biondetti's victory in the 1948 classic with a 166 Sport coupé. Ferrari was already wise to such marketing opportunities, even if his main love was racing. He was also conscious that customers preferred even a racing car to look good, and the 166MM was nothing if not beautiful. It had a 'barchetta' body by Touring of Milan – literally meaning 'little boat'. It not only set a style that would serve Ferrari for many years but it was also much copied, notably in the AC Ace and via the Ace even in the Cobra.

Underpinning the good looks was the sort of engineering Ferrari was already becoming famous for. The chassis was a massive oval tubular frame based on a central cruciform with smaller side tubes, a layout unique to Ferrari. The suspension used simple cart-springs at the rear with parallel trailing arms on each side, and front wishbones with a transverse leaf spring. The brakes were large aluminium drums with iron liners. Supporting the body was Touring's patented 'Superleggera' construction, comprising a framework of very light tubes.

In the MM, the all-aluminium 2-litre Colombo V12 gave some 150bhp on triple Weber carburettors, at a free-revving 7500rpm. It drove through a five-speed gearbox.

Alongside other road cars of the day it was a remarkable specification, and it gave equally remarkable performance; the racing version was claimed to be good for around 140mph (225kph). It was a prolific winner. As well as the 1948 Mille Miglia that gave the MM its name, the 166 had also won the 1948 Targa Florio; 166MMs won both those races again in 1949, and crowned that with Ferrari's first Le Mans win, driven by Luigi Chinetti and Lord Selsdon. Another MM was second.

As quickly as that, Ferrari had become a major force in international racing and had sowed the seeds for an equally successful future as a road car manufacturer. From just a couple of each earlier model, almost fifty 166Ms in two series were built in all, of which around twenty-five were barchettas, the rest including five berlinettas by Touring, one spyder and one coupé by Vignale, and one 'Panoramica' berlinetta by Zagato.

The first series had taken Ferrari up to late 1951, the second series lasted through to 1953, but by that time Ferrari was already moving inexorably on. By 1950 he had taken the Colombo engine a stage further to 2.3 litres, more power and still more versions, including some very elegant Inters for the wealthy road enthusiast. And even as the 195 was surpassing the 166, the 212 was overtaking the 195. Ferrari was on his way.

166
INTER

Alongside the beautiful little 166MM 'barchetta' at the 1948 Turin Show, Enzo Ferrari showed a somewhat different sort of car. It was a good-looking four-window coupé, styled and built, as was the barchetta, by coachbuilder Touring, of Milan. It had another version of the latest 2-litre V12 and a broadly similar chassis, although it was on a slightly longer wheelbase.

This was a big move for Ferrari. Turin 1948 was the first motor show at which he'd ever exhibited, and the second Touring-bodied car at that show was also breaking new ground for the company, towards a real production model.

It was the way he knew he had to go, to pay for the racing that was his first love. The first car he ever sold to a customer was the first 166 Spyder Corsa, built in 1948 and sold to one Gabriele Besana. It was in effect only the fourth Ferrari built; before it, in 1947, there had been two 125 Sports and two 159s, but one of the 159s had in reality been nothing more than the first 1½-litre 125 with the bigger 1.9-litre engine fitted.

Having sold one car, Ferrari now started to sell one or two more, piecemeal at first, and apparently only when he had to pay either the wages or his racing expenses. One of the next went to Gabriele Besana's brother Count Soave

Besana, who finished sixth in the 1948 Mille Miglia (as won by Biondetti's 166), third in the Dolomite Gold Cup (partnered by his brother), and second in the Circuit of Posillipo in Naples.

Another of the 166 Corsas, used by Luigi Chinetti to win the Paris 12-Hour race at Montlhèry in September 1948 and then to set a number of long distance records at the same circuit, was sold to Briggs Cunningham and became the first Ferrari to be raced in the USA. Through 1948 and 1949 the racing 166s, especially the barchetta-bodied MMs, were by far the quickest 2-litre sports cars in the world, latterly probably the fastest sports car in the world full-stop. That could only have been good for business.

Still, Ferrari pursued sales with grumpy reluctance. In a small brochure produced during 1948, he listed four distinct types of car, all variants on the 2-litre 166. Two were specifically racing cars: the 166 Formula 2 was a single-seater with a 155bhp three-carburettor engine, in a derivative of the Grand Prix chassis, with independent rear suspension by swing axles; the 166MM was the aforementioned barchetta, with 140bhp three-carburettor engine and a claimed maximum speed of 136mph (218kph).

The other two cars in the brochure were more clearly

Stabilimenti Farina's version of the 166 Inter (overleaf) was on a slightly shorter chassis than the first Touring versions and rather chunkier in appearance, clearly reflecting Pinin's earlier Cisitalia 202 shape.

Although several stylists clothed early Inters, and hardly any two cars were identical, a theme emerged in the large, almost square grille (far left). Many Inters used alloy-rimmed, steel-centred Cabo Sport wheels by Borrani (below).

'touring' models; the 166 Sport was described as being fitted with a single-carburettor 89bhp engine, and it had a four-seater body by Touring, on a long, 103½-inch (2628mm) wheelbase; the final brochure car was the Allemano-bodied two-seater coupé, with 110bhp three-carburettor engine, the car with which Biondetti had actually won the 1948 Mille Miglia.

Ferrari described this last one as the 166 Inter, which was a name he had used briefly on some of the later 166 Spyder Corsas.

The new Touring-bodied coupé at Turin was also presented as a 166 Inter, but it was neither one of the Spyder Corsas nor the Biondetti coupé as shown in the brochure; rather it looked for all the world like what the brochure had listed as the 166 Sport.

In fact it *was* a variation on what Ferrari had until now called the Sport, but as the Inter it would nominally take over that car's 'production' role alongside the 166MM and the racers. At the same time, it would move another step nearer to being a true touring car than the spartan, multi-purpose Sport had been. If Ferrari had set out to be confusing, he was doing a fine job.

Whatever the name though, for a tolerably civilised road car the four-windowed Touring coupé had all the right credentials. Its all drum-braked chassis, while keeping the independent-front/live axle-rear layout, was slightly modified from earlier 166s in that it gained substantial oval-section cross-members (further to reinforce the normal cruciform-braced ladder), plus some new small-diameter side-members along the outer ends of the new cross-members, below the doors. Although virtually all the cars would go to drive-on-the-right markets, all were built with right-hand drive, like the racing models which normally, of course, ran on clockwise circuits.

The bodywork was built to Touring's patented 'Super-leggera' system, a lightweight alternative to the standard model of metal panels over a wooden frame, in this case with the thin, hand-formed aluminium panels on a light tubular superstructure built upwards from the actual chassis.

On the longer wheelbase and with quite a tall roofline, the first 166 Inter coupé had at least notional space for two occasional rear seats, and it was light and comparatively spacious, although of course it still only had two doors.

It had a single-Weber-carburetted version of the 2-litre Colombo V12 engine, with the carb on a new heated inlet manifold. It drove through a non-synchronised five-speed gearbox, so the little luxuries obviously had to stop somewhere. Ferrari claimed a modest 90bhp for this engine (in line with the suspiciously similar looking model that had appeared in that early brochure as the 166 Sport), and a top speed just a little short of 100mph (160kph). Today, that might not sound like much for a Ferrari but in 1948 it was suitably impressive.

So the Inter went on sale as Ferrari's first purpose-built road car and it did quite well. The numbers, of course, were tiny but the die was cast. It established a pattern for the foreseeable future, too, of Ferrari simply supplying the rolling chassis and the customer worrying about the coach-work. That is why virtually no two early Ferraris, even ones with supposedly identical specifications, really look exactly the same.

In the case of the 166 Inter, most of the customers (eventually numbering almost forty) went to the company who had styled the first car – Touring. There were all the usual detail variations, but also three distinct series. Late in 1949, they gave the car a more modern look by continuing the wing line straight through from front to rear, with a strong, straight, styling line, rather than one alluding (as the original had) to the old-fashioned swoopy separation. At Turin in 1950 they added a new shape in the form of a full-length roofline; what we might now call a fastback.

Normal equipment behind any of the various styles of grille (top) and bonnet scoop (centre) was a mild, single-carburettor V12. Most windscreens (centre) used flat glass and centre split. Farina's 'fastback' rear window (above) was tiny.

**166 INTER
SPECIFICATION**

ENGINE
60° V12

CAPACITY
1995cc

BORE x STROKE
60.0 x 58.8mm

COMPRESSION RATIO
7.5:1

POWER
110bhp

VALVE GEAR
Single overhead camshafts

FUEL SYSTEM
Single Weber 32DCF carburettor

TRANSMISSION
Five-speed manual

FRONT SUSPENSION
Independent, by double wishbones, transverse leaf spring, lever dampers

REAR SUSPENSION
Non-independent, by live axle, semi-elliptic leaf springs, parallel arms, lever dampers

BRAKES
All drums

WHEELS
Centre-lock alloy/steel; wires optional

WEIGHT
c.1760lb (798kg)

MAXIMUM SPEED
c.105mph (168kph)

NUMBER MADE, DATES
c.38, 1948–51

Early in 1949, at Geneva (which was Ferrari's first show appearance outside of Italy), there was a 166 Inter with cabriolet body by Stabilimenti Farina. It was Farina's second Ferrari and Ferrari's first cabrio, implying the inclusion of a soft-top, as distinct from the simple, open-topped spyders and barchettas; it was another early sign of Ferrari giving the customers what they wanted. Farina built two more 166 Inter cabrios, both quite different, and they also bodied four coupés.

Ghia and Bertone offered one car apiece, a coupé from the former, a cabrio from the latter, and in both cases their first work on Ferrari chassis. The other main styling house for 166 Inters was newcomer Vignale, who had only gone into business on his own account in 1946 after leaving Farina, but who was already vying with Touring for most of Ferrari's work. Vignale built nine very attractive coupés and one cabriolet and guaranteed himself a good deal of patronage for the future, until Pinin Farina came along.

In May 1949, three 166 Inter coupés (all with different bodies) proved that they could race too, with a clean sweep in the Coppa Inter-Europa, a race for what we would now call GT cars; that was an interesting sideline, but the real importance of the 166 Inter was in establishing the commercial line. They were succeeded by the 195 Inter in 1951, but the 195 was more a continuation of the theme than a replacement.

195
INTER

Over the years, through both his racing and his road car dealings, Enzo Ferrari built himself a notable reputation for stubborn individuality and aloofness. His treatment of customers, even racing customers with whom you might reasonably have expected him to have some kind of empathy, was legendary – rarely better than disinterested, often pointedly rude.

Many and consistent are the stories of visitors to Maranello, even rich and famous ones with cash in hand to collect their new car, being kept waiting and fuming, often for hours. Sometimes they made it as far as the tiny anteroom, occasionally they weren't even allowed beyond the front gates and had to await the call in the restaurant over the road. Anyone who came to the shrine-like factory to have a car repaired risked being treated like a man who had abused Ferrari's personal property, not his own; anyone who came to request modifications would like as not be treated with utmost contempt for such presumption.

Strangely for a man who had once wanted to be a journalist, who manipulated the press for all it was worth in many respects, and who when the mood took him could be warmly urbane and witty, Enzo Ferrari seemed to have a peculiarly off-hand way of treating that normally symbiotic relationship. He was a notoriously hard man to interview, almost totally disinclined to let anyone other than a potential owner test his creations, and a good proportion of what early road tests there are talk of cars with astonishingly poor preparation and below-par performance.

Given his scant interest in the commercial side of the business, and his almost theatrical feel for promoting a Ferrari mystique beyond the cars, that was explicable if not forgivable, but his studied awkwardness extended to several aspects of his racing too. After the early days, with very few exceptions, he refused to travel to races, preferring to run operations from his office, with his generals reporting back from the field by telephone – and woe betide them if the news was poor. It was an almost sadistically clever way of domineering his minions.

And he was infuriatingly unwilling to accept change, as evidenced over the years by his lateness in racing to follow

Before his pact with Pinin Farina, Ferrari left his customers to choose their coachbuilder. Vignale had worked for Farina and only been in business for a few years on his own, but his 195 Inter (left and far left) shows a fine touch.

Vignale, and especially his young stylist Michelotti, was more than willing to add a touch of flamboyance, even a toned-down version of late-1940s Detroit-style frippery, to his creations (overleaf) yet they rarely lost their basic elegance.

such proven advances as disc brakes, monocoque chassis and mid-engines. Again, it was a philosophical stance; in the Ferrari philosophy it was engines that won races and his engines were the best in the world.

Even the best engines in the world, though, must get better to stay ahead of the opposition. Motor racing is a constant quest for power; power wins races, and all other things being equal, more capacity means more power. When Ferrari came onto the scene in the late 1940s with his spectacularly advanced V12 engine and all-new chassis, he had the huge advantage of having one of the few really up-to-date cars in racing, and built a lot of his early reputation against frankly mediocre opposition. But that didn't last for long and Ferrari continued to win on merit.

Leaving the chassis largely unchanged allowed Ferrari to pursue that obsession with engines for all that it was worth. Look at the first five years of Ferrari history and you will see the astonishing rate of progress; in 1947 there was the 1½-litre 125 and the 1.9-litre 159, in 1948 the 2-litre 166, in 1950 the 2.3-litre 195; by the beginning of 1951 there was the 2½-litre 212 and in 1952 the 2.7-litre 225 provided the last link to the classic 3-litre 250.

Concurrent Lampredi development apart, all that progression was based on the original Colombo engine, and once

the stroke had been fixed at 58.8mm in the 166, all the capacity increases came from relatively simple increases in bore size, made possible by the generous bore spacing built in at the earliest design stage.

On that basis, it would be easy to dismiss the 195 as just one fleeting interim stage between 166 and 212, but it was important in its role as a car to consolidate the progress. Before the 166, Ferrari had made nothing but racing cars in tiny numbers and his reputation actually rested on little more than admittedly considerable domestic racing success. With the Le Mans winning, Mille Miglia winning, Targa Florio winning 166, Ferrari established worldwide fame and opened up a 'production-car' market; with the 195 he kept up the momentum.

The first manifestation of the 195 was in racing, in 1950, in the 195 Sport. The extra capacity helped power to increase from about 140 to 170bhp, with good reliability because the seven main bearing V12 was actually a very lightly stressed unit. No more than a handful of this model were built, and possibly only one car that was any more than an upgrading of earlier 166s; but one did win the 1950 Mille Miglia. This was driven by Gianni Marzotto, and the same car, with Raymond Sommer at the wheel, comfortably led the 1950 Le Mans 24-Hours before being

Michelotti's work included a lot of experimentation with radiator grilles. He did the V16 BRM's, and originated the classic Ferrari oval 'egg-crate' style, but this (above and top) was more flamboyant. Inters were well trimmed too (above left).

A few years earlier, Ferrari would never have dreamed of such blatant trimmings as Vignale's stylised door trim (above, far left), elaborate two-tone colours (far left), or the ornate and quite heavy bumpers front and rear (above left and left).

195 INTER SPECIFICATION

ENGINE
60° V12

CAPACITY
2341cc

BORE x STROKE
65.0 × 58.8mm

COMPRESSION RATIO
7.5:1

POWER
135bhp

VALVE GEAR
Single overhead camshafts

FUEL SYSTEM
Single Weber 36DCF carburettor

TRANSMISSION
Five-speed manual

FRONT SUSPENSION
Independent, by double wishbones, transverse leaf spring, lever dampers

REAR SUSPENSION
Non-independent, by live axle, semi-elliptic leaf springs, parallel arms, lever dampers

BRAKES
All drums

WHEELS
Centre-lock wire

WEIGHT
c.2100lb (952kg)

MAXIMUM SPEED
c.115mph (185kph)

NUMBER MADE, DATES
c.25, 1951–2

put out of the race by mechanical problems.

Alongside the 195 Sport, following the pattern established by the 166 Inter, Ferrari soon offered a 195 Inter, a car intended more for touring than for racing and with an appropriately milder specification and more comprehensive trim and equipment. The first example seems to have been completed late in 1950, but it wasn't put on public display until January 1951, when it appeared at the Brussels Show.

Where the 195 Sport had been built on the shorter, 86.6-inch (2200mm) wheelbase of the 166MM, the 195 Inter used the 98.4-inch (2500mm) wheelbase of the 166 Inter, and in fact apart from the bigger engine there were few differences between those two models. The Inter engine was usually supplied with a single downdraught Weber carburettor, slightly bigger in the case of the 195 than on the 166, so in spite of slightly lower compression ratio, power went up from 110 to 135bhp, with a bit more available from the optional three-carburettor set-up. The chassis was pure 166, with five-speed gearbox, drum brakes, wishbone/transverse leaf front suspension and live axle rear, with lever dampers.

All the 195 Inters were bodied as coupés (which made them noticeably heavier than the barchettas that they resembled below the belt-line), with coachwork by four houses, Ghia, the unrelated Ghia-Aigle of Switzerland, Touring and Vignale; and the last of those were arguably the most accomplished, although, of course, virtually every car had styling variations.

The 195 was one of the shorter lived Ferraris, even among the early models. It stayed in production for barely a full year, during which time only around twenty-five examples were built in total, but seen in the proper perspective it was a successful model. The reason for its short career was actually there right from the day the 195 appeared in public; alongside it at that first show appearance in Brussels in January 1951, Ferrari had showed the 4.1-litre Lampredi-engined 340 America and another development of the Colombo line, very similar in most respects to the 195, and even to the 166 that that was following on from. Similar, that is, save for a yet larger version of the same engine, in this case up to a shade beyond 2.5 litres and with the label 212.

It was a 212 which outclassed the four 195 Inters that appeared in the Coppa Inter Europa, a race run for the newly fashionable GT cars, at Monza in April 1951. The 195 wasn't quite obsolete before it was built, but with the remarkable pace of development in the early years at Maranello, it was not very far off.

340
AMERICA
CABRIOLET

It would be fair to say that Enzo Ferrari astonished the motoring world when he launched his first true Ferrari cars in 1947, by the size of their complex and beautifully engineered V12 engines. But the surprise was not that the engines had followed the usual path to power and were so big, but that Ferrari had started as he then meant to go on, with highly individual and unconventional thinking, and the engines were so small for so many cylinders. Just 1½ litres in fact in the original 125s, or as the numbering scheme suggested, only 125cc per cylinder – half the cylinder size of a Fiat 500 Topolino!

These first Ferrari V12 engines were designed by Gioacchino Colombo, and their diminutive 1½-litre displacement wasn't just a touch of eccentricity on Ferrari's part, it was part of Ferrari's plan to comply with the new Grand Prix formula for cars of 4½ litres unsupercharged, or 1½ litres supercharged.

Presumably with an eye to the excellence of the straight-eight 1½-litre supercharged Alfa 158 Grand Prix engine, which Colombo had designed before being tempted away to

Maranello, Ferrari chose the small capacity, multi-cylinder route. Where the big unsupercharged engine would have been pretty much a one-purpose solution, the small engine could go Grand Prix racing with a supercharger, while without supercharging it would also give Ferrari the ability to offer a reasonably affordable customer sports car and a sports-racing model that would be adaptable for the junior single-seater classes.

In the smaller ranks, and in his fledgling 'production' cars, the beautiful and efficient little V12s were highly successful, but Roots-supercharged for Grand Prix racing, in the 1948 125GP (another variant of the early multi-purpose two-seater) and the 1949 four-cam 125F1 (Ferrari's first purpose-built Grand Prix car), it couldn't get near the dominant Alfas, now in 159 guise.

So, as he was wont occasionally to do with his protégés, Ferrari fell out with Colombo in 1950 and sent him on his way (to go first to arch-rival Maserati where he designed the 250F, later to Bugatti to design their final visionary, but unfulfilled, Grand Prix car, the mid-engined Type 251).

As well as starting a line of American-market-inspired road cars with the bigger Lampredi engines under their heavily sculpted bonnets (right), cars like the 340 America Cabriolet offered a much more luxurious image (left) than the barchettas.

Vignale and Michelotti had occasionally put American styling touches on road cars that were almost certainly going to stay in Europe, but their unique 340 America Cabriolet (above and right) offered America a classic European elegance.

At Ferrari though, Colombo's legacy remained, and his 'short-block' engine and its descendants served with distinction for virtually two decades, right up to the 3.3-litre variant in the 1966 275GTB/4.

To replace Colombo, Ferrari had Aurelio Lampredi, a designer with less obvious pedigree than Colombo, who had previously been Colombo's assistant, had left in 1947 and returned within a year. Where Colombo had been champion of the highly supercharged small capacity engine, and where that had originally been convenient for Ferrari's wider plans, for Grand Prix racing Lampredi now advocated the solution of the big unblown engine, which he reckoned could produce the power and be less thirsty. All Ferrari wanted to do now was to win, so Lampredi got his chance.

Thus started Ferrari's second classic V12 line, the Lampredi 'long-block' engines. To allow the large capacities he planned, Lampredi designed another 60° V12 but with considerably wider bore spacing than Colombo's little jewel, which of course made it markedly longer overall. It wasn't just bigger, though; the wet cylinder liners were now screwed into the cylinder head faces for better gas sealing, there were roller rocker arms and individual rather than siamesed inlet ports, and the lubrication system was quite different.

At first, the big Lampredi engine was intended purely for racing, because at this early stage Ferrari saw little scope in selling such big (and by extension expensive) sports cars to his 'touring' customers. It appeared first in 1950, a 3.3-litre form in two 275S racing sports cars for the Mille Miglia, and again as a 3.3-litre in a 125F1 chassis in the Belgian Grand Prix in June. Enlarged to 4.1 litres it was entered in a new chassis for the Grand Prix des Nations in Geneva in July, and finally in September, appropriately enough in the Italian Grand Prix at Monza, it appeared as a

Exceptionally strong and light Borrani wire wheels (above left) were a long-standing Ferrari hallmark and the epitome of European sports car styling, while Vignale excelled at detail touches like the distinctive door handle (above).

With the big Lampredi engine to feed and cool, and maybe with California in mind, the 340's bonnet (left) gained a long cold-air scoop to get the air to the carburettors, and some generous slots to let the heat out from around the engine compartment.

full 4½-litre Grand Prix engine, in the 375F1. It gave Ferrari the success he desperately needed, beating the Alfa 159 fair and square at the British Grand Prix at Silverstone in 1951. He didn't build another supercharged Grand Prix engine until the turbo 1½-litre 126C of 1980.

Back in the hard commercial world though, Ferrari was hardly making his fortune in the early days; in fact he was only barely surviving. Winning races as diverse as the Mille Miglia, Le Mans and now Grands Prix was all well and good, but he still had to sell customer cars to pay the bills; and Europe, still recovering from the war, simply wasn't buying enough. After the 1949 Le Mans win though, America started to take notice of Ferrari, and that was a whole different market.

The 1949 Le Mans winner had been driven almost single-handedly by one Luigi Chinetti, a former winner for Alfa Romeo who now lived in New York and sold cars.

Chinetti persuaded his old friend Ferrari to let him sell *his* cars in the USA and as soon as they started winning races in America, with its new-found interest in European-style road racing, Ferrari never looked back.

That, in a nutshell, is how the big Lampredi engines started to find their way into the road cars as well as the racers and how Ferrari expanded his whole philosophy. Because the inescapable fact was that although Americans now had a bit more of an understanding of the small but nimble European sports cars for the racing circuits, deep down they still believed in cubic inches. In the Lampredi engines, Ferrari could now give the customer interested in fast and stylish grand touring exactly what was ordered.

The 340 America, powered by a 220bhp 4.1-litre version of the Lampredi engine, mated to a five-speed gearbox, was unveiled at the Paris Show in October 1950, just a month after the 375F1's Monza debut. The show car

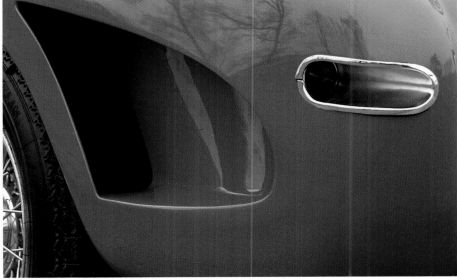

The one-off Cabriolet was not unlike a sleeker version of Vignale's drophead 195 Inter. It had its bumperless nose raked steeply forwards (above left), and its tail lamps (above) wrapped around an even lower and even more curvaceous rear end (left).

340 AMERICA CABRIOLET SPECIFICATION

ENGINE
60° V12

CAPACITY
4102cc

BORE x STROKE
70.0 × 68.0mm

COMPRESSION RATIO
8.0:1

POWER
220bhp

VALVE GEAR
Single overhead camshafts

FUEL SYSTEM
Three Weber 40DCF carburettors

TRANSMISSION
Five-speed manual

FRONT SUSPENSION
Independent, by double wishbones, transverse leaf spring, lever dampers

REAR SUSPENSION
Non-independent, by live axle, semi-elliptic leaf springs, parallel arms, lever dampers

BRAKES
All drums

WHEELS
Centre-lock wire

WEIGHT
c.2000lb (907kg)

MAXIMUM SPEED
c.140mph (225kph)

NUMBER MADE, DATES
c.25, 1951

was a barchetta, by Touring, with a typical Ferrari chassis using transverse-leaf and wishbone independent front suspension and live axle rear suspension. The two 275S barchettas that had introduced the Lampredi engine in 3.3-litre form but had failed to finish the 1950 Mille Miglia, were both given 4.1-litre engines and became 240 Americas, and Ferrari began to build the 340 in series.

It was only a relatively short series admittedly, but it was a new start. A couple of dozen were built, with a wide range of body styles from barchetta to berlinetta, by Ghia, Touring and Vignale. Ferrari saw them principally as a racing model, and several were given more powerful, dry-sumped engines. Although some stayed in Europe, a number did go to America.

In 1952 a few cars were uprated for the prestigious Carrera Panamericana road race, as 340 Mexicos, and in 1953 Ferrari made an even more powerful variant, as the 340MM. That duly won the event it was named for, the Mille Miglia, before growing up into the 375MM. In 1952, the 340 America itself was replaced by a new car, similar in its basics but with its sights more firmly on road use, as the 342 America. It sat on a slightly longer, wider chassis, had four rather than five gears, and slightly less power from a similar 4.1-litre engine. It wasn't a great success, because even America didn't want an overbodied and underpowered Ferrari, and only a handful were built.

Ferrari's next attack on the US market, the 375 America as launched in Paris in 1953, gained almost half a litre and 100bhp over the unfortunate 342. In essence, it was a big-engined version of the 250 Europa, geared to American tastes. Again, it sold in tiny numbers, just a dozen before it was replaced in 1955 by the 410 Superamerica, which gave America even more of what it wanted and ultimately led to the Superfast. Ferrari was learning.

212
INTER

One of the most oft-quoted Ferrari-isms is the Ingegnere's reply to the impossible question 'which is your favourite car?'. Ferrari, ever the clever diplomat and marketing man, had a stock answer to that one, and no matter how often he was asked the question over the years his response was always some variation on the theme of 'the one I will build tomorrow'.

It wasn't entirely glib or dismissive; in large part he meant it because so far as his cars were concerned sentiment for the past held little appeal for Ferrari in comparison with ambition for the future. That may be one reason why he was so successful so soon, and why the early years of his company, while being so precarious financially, were so rich technically.

Put simply, once he had gone into business, Ferrari could not afford to stand still; fortunately he wasn't afraid to change. His market was rarefied, certainly, but it was by no means a sinecure. There were the likes of Alfa Romeo, Maserati and Aston, of Jaguar, Mercedes, Lancia and, increasingly, Porsche to compete against. By the standards of some of those companies, Ferrari was not only a newcomer, he was also a minnow among the big fish.

So if Ferrari always thought his products technically superior, he had to prove it through racing, and to pay for the racing he had to sell customer cars.

Against that background, the commercial side of his fledgling company had to face the reality of growing up. By 1950 two separate lines of thought were evident in Ferrari's road cars, in Colombo's short-block and Lampredi's long-block engines. The Lampredi design had been introduced principally for racing, in the 275S sports model and then in Grand Prix form, and by 1951 it had been adopted for the road in the first 4.1-litre 340 America; but the main thrust of Ferrari's 'production' models was still through the Colombo V12 family.

Having started with the 1½-litre 125s in 1947, by 1951 the Colombo-powered Ferraris had already evolved through the interim 1.9-litre 159, introduced later in the same year, to the 2-litre 166 in 1948, and the 2.4-litre 195s from 1950. From the 166 on, the stroke of the engine was set, at 58.8mm, and there it stayed while Ferrari juggled the capacity ever higher by progressively increasing the bore, right through to the final flowering of the seminal Colombo design, the 3.3-litre 275 of the mid-1960s.

Later, especially within the long-running 250 family,

Vignale bodied most of the 212 Inters but the cars still varied markedly and only three of this type (far left) were built. Right-hand drive (above) was about to disappear and stylish door handle (left) shows this was more than just a racer.

Ferrari introduced other refinements, notably in the chassis, but in the early days, uprating the capacity and power yet again didn't automatically imply any other great changes between models.

The 2.6-litre 212, as first seen at the Brussels Show in 1951, was a good example of that steady but cautious development. The 212 was launched in two main versions, the Export and the Inter; the Export was intended for competition (or at least as a dual-purpose road/race car),

while the lower-tuned Inter was intended solely as a reasonably fast and of course quite exclusive tourer.

As such, the 212 was an obvious follow on from the 195 of 1950 (in which the two versions had been labelled Sport and Inter), and in turn from the 166, which had been the first Ferrari to introduce the 'Inter' concept, alongside the Sport, Corsa and MM racing models back in 1948.

Rationalising the output to just Inter and Export series helped Ferrari make the most of limited resources yet still satisfy two markets. Although specifications of individual cars varied markedly, the main mechanical difference between the two cars in the 212's case was that the Export had trible Weber carburettors, the Inter initially had just the one. There were other minor differences; the Inter had a rather lower compression ratio than the Export, for instance – presumably because a car intended for touring occasionally had to accept whatever inferior grade of fuel it could get while the racing model was usually in a position to be much better fed. So initially the Inter produced only 150bhp where the Export produced as much as 165, but that was further confused in 1952, when the Inter adopted revised cylinder heads plus the Export's three-carb set-up to improve to 170bhp, more on a par with the Export, which

The 212 Inter on the longer chassis was a big car (left) but Vignale gave it a sporty aggression with the low roof and huge grille. A central bonnet ridge on this car (above) led to two badges for symmetry. As a tourer, it had its limits (top).

rather than being wrung out for more horsepower was to be superseded by the 255s and the 250s.

As well as the engine differences, the Inters generally had longer wheelbase chassis than the Exports – as much as 13½ inches difference, in fact, between the shortest Export barchetta and the normal Inter berlinetta. Otherwise, the chassis are much the same, and the 212 is no more than a fairly simple continuation of the 166 and 195 line. That means the chassis still follow the simple but effective early Ferrari pattern of a tubular ladder frame with cross bracing; independent front suspension is by unequal length upper and lower wishbones acting on lower transverse leaf spring, while the rear uses a live axle on cart springs, with parallel trailing arms for better location. There was one quite important chassis change in 1952, when Ferrari changed the 212s from the racing-inspired right-hand drive format he had preferred up to now to left-hand drive, which was more logical for most of his touring-car markets.

The 212s in fact built a fine racing record. In 1951 a 212 driven by Pagnibon and Barraquet won the first Tour de France, an event that Ferrari was to dominate for many years with his 'dual-purpose' GT cars. In the same year, Marzotto and Taruffi were first and second with 212 Exports in the Tour of Sicily, and Villoresi won the Coppa Inter-Europa at Monza. But the most important result came when a pair of Vignale-bodied 212 Export coupés driven by Taruffi/Chinetti and Villoresi/Ascari were first and second in the 1951 Carrera Panamericana. Ferrari would mainly offer his bigger engined cars to America, but the role of that win in convincing the US market of Ferrari's credentials was far greater and far more important than any number of European victories.

That said, the vast majority of 212s did stay in Europe and a large proportion (some eighty of the 110 or so built) were Inters not Exports. They included an amazing variety of styles from many *carrozzerie*. Some were a little heavy-handed in their detail and chrome-laden decoration, but many were exceptionally handsome, and the 212 marked a significant turning point in Ferrari's preferred coachbuilders. First to body the Inter was Vignale (at the time employing Giovanni Michelotti), and there were early cars from Touring and Ghia. The most prolific was Vignale, who made Inter cabriolets and coupés (plus Export cabrios, berlinettas and spyders) in some six recognisably different series up to his final coupé style introduced in March 1953; but the most far reaching addition to the stylists was Pinin Farina, who bodied a road Ferrari for the first time.

Battista (nickname 'Pinin') Farina was the younger brother of Giovanni Farina, the great stylist whose Stabilimenti Farina (founded in 1905) had bodied just a few Ferraris in the early days. Late in 1952 Stabilimenti Farina bodied a 212 Inter coupé, their last Ferrari, before the company went out of business. Touring faded away with one final 212 Inter barchetta in 1952, and Vignale departed with a last run of 212 Inter coupés.

Meanwhile, 'Pinin' (Battista officially changed his surname and the name of his company to Pininfarina in 1958) bodied a 212 Inter cabriolet which was sold in Switzerland

in 1952. In January 1953 a Pinin Farina 212 Inter coupé was shown in Brussels and Pinin went on to body three Inter cabrios and some fourteen or fifteen coupés. Within a year he was clothing virtually all Ferrari's production for both road and track.

Appropriately perhaps, the last of the 212 Inters was a Pinin Farina coupé, built in 1953, after which the model was superseded by the Lampredi-engined 250 Europa 375 America. Its true spiritual successor didn't arrive until 1954; when it did appear, it was in the guise of the 250GT Europa, foundation of the 250 dynasty.

Elegance was creeping into the Ferrari vocabulary with the success of the Inters, inside (above) as in the beautifully detailed door panels, and out (top) in Michelotti's neat tail lamp treatment. Three carbs (centre) were an option.

The two-tone paintwork on this example emphasises the long, low, almost fastback roofline (left) and many Inters were two-colour. The clever spring (below) kept the boot lid raised, another touch of consideration for the roadgoing customer.

**212 INTER
SPECIFICATION**

ENGINE
60° V12

CAPACITY
2563cc

BORE x STROKE
68.0 x 58.8mm

COMPRESSION RATIO
8.0:1

POWER
150bhp (later 170bhp)

VALVE GEAR
Single overhead camshafts

FUEL SYSTEM
Single Weber 36DCF carburettor (later three 36DCFs)

TRANSMISSION
Five-speed manual

FRONT SUSPENSION
Independent, by double wishbones, transverse leaf spring, lever dampers

REAR SUSPENSION
Non-independent, by live axle, semi-elliptic leaf springs, parallel arms, lever dampers

BRAKES
All drums

WHEELS
Centre-lock wire

WEIGHT
c.2250lb (1020kg)

MAXIMUM SPEED
c.125mph (201kph)

NUMBER MADE, DATES
c.84, 1951–2

250MM

He obviously couldn't have known it at the time, but in 1952 when he upgraded the already departed Colombo's versatile V12 from the 2.6 litres of the 212 series, via the 2.7 litres of the short run of 225S competition cars, to the full 3 litres of the first 250 models, Ferrari all but guaranteed the future of his company.

It was less than six years since the motoring press had announced that the former racing driver, former Alfa team manager intended to become a constructor under his own name; barely five years since he had launched his astonishingly complex 1½-litre V12 cars just as promised, and shown that far from being pipe dreams they were carefully thought through and quite capable of winning in all manner of racing.

In 1948, Ferraris won the Mille Miglia and the Targa Florio. In 1949 they repeated both those wins and added the big one, Le Mans, for the first time. On the other side of the Atlantic in 1949, Briggs Cunningham won at Watkins Glen in the first Ferrari imported into America. In 1951 a Ferrari won the Mille Miglia again, plus the Carrera Panamericana, a gruelling 2000-mile marathon in South America which many people thought made European road races look like a picnic. Ferraris were already winning Grand Prix races, and starting to become a household word wherever sporting cars were appreciated.

Reporting that first Le Mans win in July 1949, *The Autocar* remarked, 'Although production is numbered in tens rather than hundreds, the 2-litre Ferrari is offered in a range of types that would do credit to a factory turning out a thousand a day. When Enzo Ferrari . . . hired Ing. Colombo to design the most advanced 2-litre car yet seen, he worked on the assumption that the customer is always right, especially if he has from two to five thousand pounds to spend . . . '

That compliment hid Enzo Ferrari's dilemma. He was winning fame but the one thing he wasn't doing was making his fortune.

By 1951, the story hadn't improved much, not on the commercial side. In June the same magazine commented 'Exploits in Grand Prix and sports car racing have won world fame for Ferrari cars in a very short time; but very few people can speak with first hand knowledge of their capabilities. Being individually made, they are very expensive, and the total number of cars built so far is probably under three hundred.' Yet the works were large, modern

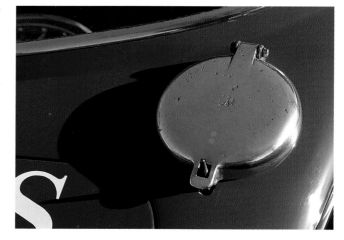

Even without the sign writing, the massive quick-action fuel-filler cap (left) and the scatter of cooling and engine-breathing vents around the front end (below) are certain signs that this is a car with competition in mind.

and well-equipped, and the workforce, by the very nature of the hand-built product, was both large and skilled. According to *The Motor* in 1951, the quality control section alone had some thirty foremen and inspectors. It took around a fortnight to build and test an engine, 2500 man-hours to build a sports car, 3500 to 4000 hours to build a racing car — without design and development time. There were some forty specialists in the racing department.

The total monthly output, on the other hand, was twenty-five to thirty cars, racers included. It only barely added up.

The 250 series, fortunately, was to prove the turning point for Ferrari, the cars that finally turned him from a sometimes struggling producer of one-offs and small runs to a more substantial and financially secure manufacturer.

Most 250MMs were berlinettas by Pinin Farina, and Vignale bodied a number of spyders, but this coupé by Vignale is unique. With the US market opening up, a stylist as astute as Vignale couldn't miss the early '50s theme of vestigial fins (right).

Centre-lock wire wheels were
traditional fare for Ferrari
through the '50s and into the
'60s (left) and for longer
than most they covered drum
brakes. One choke per
cylinder, courtesy of Weber
(below), marks a full-race
version of the 250 engine.

The 250 family grew and continued for a full decade, and
by the end of its run that total production figure had risen
from *The Autocar*'s 1951 estimate of less than 300, to nearer
3500 cars.

The first of the 250s was the 250S racing sports car,
which appeared in public around March 1952. In its turn,
the 250S was a development of the earlier 225S, another
1952 design, with a 2.7-litre, 210bhp Colombo engine. Or
more correctly, a Colombo engine with a number of
Lampredi features, such as roller cam followers and individual rather than siamesed inlet tracts. The 225S was one
of Ferrari's more successful models, as a prolific race winner
and with a production run of some twenty cars (Vignale
spyders and berlinettas and one barchetta by Touring), but
of course Ferrari was already looking to the next stage.

That inevitably meant another increase in capacity. For
the 250, the stroke was left as for the 225 engine, at

Ferrari won the gruelling
Carrera Panamericana in 1951
with a Vignale-bodied 212
coupé and in 1954 with the
Lampredi-engined 375 Plus,
but although the 250MM was a
natural Carrera challenger
(left) in private hands, it
never won the race itself.

43

58.8mm, while the bore was increased again, from 70.0 to 73.0mm. That gave a capacity of 2953cc. For the original Colombo engine that was as far as it could go – a full 3 litres was exactly double the size of the engine as it had first appeared. It was now an ideal size, big enough for both marketing and racing purposes, with the desirable combination of large piston area and short stroke to produce ample power and free-revving flexibility, yet still with the compactness and light weight of the short block. With appropriate carburation, camshafts and tuning, it was versatile enough to suit every species of 250 from tourer to world championship sports racer. With some justification, the classic Colombo 3-litre became the longest running and most successful of all Ferrari engines.

The one-off 250S, which was really no more than a Vignale-bodied 225S berlinetta with the new 3-litre engine, had a short but glorious career. It led Le Mans but failed to finish; it also led much of the Carrera Panamericana until retiring with transmission failure; it won the Pescara 12-hour race; but the most famous victory of all had already been scored, earlier in the year, in the 1952 Mille Miglia. The 'Thousand Miles' is one of the hardest of all road races, and in this case was against exceptionally tough competition. Giovanni Bracco (the Pescara winner and Carrera leader) was the driver, and he beat the works Mercedes-Benz 300SL of Karl Kling into second place, with a display of astonishingly aggressive driving.

Ferrari seized his opportunity with characteristic flair. At the Paris Show in October 1952 he showed a new model (in chassis form only) which he called the 250MM – 250 for

By the time the 250 had appeared, Ferrari had stopped bucking the trend and adopted left-hand drive (left) as the norm, but the general interior feel still put racing first. The coupé roofline distinguishes it from a berlinetta (above).

Extraction vents moulded into the rear quarter windows (above) and long bonnet-scoop (left), served broadly similar purposes – to keep the driver and the engine respectively supplied with cool air and working at peak efficiency . . .

250MM SPECIFICATION

ENGINE
60° V12

CAPACITY
2953cc

BORE x STROKE
73.0 x 58.8mm

COMPRESSION RATIO
9.0:1

POWER
240bhp

VALVE GEAR
Single overhead camshafts

FUEL SYSTEM
Three Weber 36IF4C carburettors

TRANSMISSION
Four-speed manual

FRONT SUSPENSION
Independent, by double wishbones, transverse leaf spring, lever dampers

REAR SUSPENSION
Non-independent, by live axle, semi-elliptic leaf springs, parallel arms, lever dampers

BRAKES
All drums

WHEELS
Centre-lock wire

WEIGHT
c.2350lb (1065kg)

MAXIMUM SPEED
c.155mph (249kph)

NUMBER MADE, DATES
c.36, 1952–3

the now proven new engine, and MM for Bracco's Mille Miglia victory. It had the main chassis dimensions and engine features of the 250S, with its roller camshaft followers and 12-port cylinder heads. Power output on a three-Weber carburettor engine was now quoted as 240bhp, and that was transmitted through a four-speed syncromesh gearbox in unit with the engine, where the 250S had had a five-speed crash type. It was a much easier gearchange to use, with a lighter action than the unsynchronised type, and it was typical of the new emphasis on refinement that Ferrari would steadily move towards.

Of the three dozen or so 250MMs built during 1952 and 1953, just over half were Pinin Farina bodied berlinettas, followed by almost as many Vignale spyders and a single coupé also generally attributed to Vignale.

A little surprisingly perhaps, the works didn't have any great racing success with the 250MM, and in particular it hardly lived up to its name in the 1952 Mille Miglia, where none of the three works-entered cars even finished. For privateers, though, the 250MMs were the car to have for GT racing in 1953 and 1954 as the race wins accumulated on both sides of the Atlantic; and winning races on a Sunday sold cars on a Monday – even Ferrari.

After one brief abberation in the form of the 250 Europa (a 3-litre Lampredi-engined car based on the longer wheelbase 375 America) Ferrari launched into the 250 series proper in 1954 with the 250GT Europa, Colombo engine, four-speed syncro gearbox and all. It launched those two little letters 'GT' into the Ferrari lexicon, and with the magic numbers 250, they were the start of something very special.

250GT
EUROPA

Of every car in the Ferrari catalogue the 250GT Europa, in retrospect, is perhaps the most important, as the real foundation of the classic 250 family which made Ferrari's fortune through the 1950s and 1960s. Ferrari introduced it late in 1954 at the Paris Show. It quickly came to be known as the 'second series' 250 Europa, and initially Ferrari's literature described it simply as another 250 Europa, but more correctly it was the 250*GT* Europa, and that name was soon adopted officially. It is easily confused with, but was in fact very different from, the earlier 250 Europa, and nowadays it is the car that most people consider to be Ferrari's first true production model.

The original 250 Europa (retrospectively known as the first series) had been introduced in Paris in October 1953, on the longest chassis used by Ferrari up to that time, with a 110.2-inch wheelbase. That reflected the fact that the first 250 Europa (as opposed to 'second series' 250GT Europa) was essentially a smaller-engined cousin to the 300bhp, 4½-litre 375 America. That in turn was another

new model, launched at the same 1953 Paris Show, and it was a big, powerful GT car which represented Ferrari's next attack on the potentially lucrative US market.

The 250 Europa at the 1953 Paris Show was a coupé by Vignale, but Vignale only went on to clothe two coupés in the 250 Europa series, and two coupés and a cabrio in the 375 America series, between 1953 and 1954 in the case of the Europa, and 1953 and 1955 in the case of the America. The vast majority of the approximately seventeen 250 Europas and thirteen 375 Americas made were bodied by Pinin Farina, who was already developing a special relationship with Ferrari as his 'in-house' body builder.

Farina's bodies for the 250 Europa and the 275 America looked virtually identical. They were simple in appearance and very close to uniform in execution, save for detail differences in the roofline and window layouts. In each case, they were extremely nice looking cars — softly rounded, with low roofline, long, low bonnet, and large, almost vertical, 'egg-crate' oval grille, which itself established a long-running pattern.

The 250GT Europa meant not just a new model but a new philosophy, practical enough to be a tourer, quick enough to be a racer. Inside (left) were full instruments and a four-speed gearchange, outside (right) was a new uniformity by Pinin Farina.

The wraparound rear window style (above) of the 250GT Europa was a clear carry-over from the 250 Europa, and so was the overall shape (right), but the wheelbase was shorter, the chassis heavily modified and the handling much improved.

The 250GT Europa, the 'second series' as launched in Paris in October 1954, also looked all but identical to the Pinin Farina 250s and 375s, but it was a totally different car under the skin.

Both the 250 Europa and the 375 America had used Lampredi-type, 'long-block' engines. The 4½-litre made the most of the big-block layout with 84.0mm bores, but the 3-litre engine of the Lampredi-type 250 had bore and stroke dimensions of 68.0 x 68.0mm, which made it one of the few exactly 'square' engines that Ferrari ever built. But the problem with the 250 Europa was that, good as the big Lampredi engine was in its full-capacity forms, as a 3-litre it wasn't nearly as good as the superbly compact and powerful Colombo-type engine, being at the same time bigger, heavier but unfortunately *less* powerful.

The Colombo engine, on the other hand, had already

grown to twice the 1½-litre size at which it was launched and even at that stretch had convincingly proved both its power and reliability in racing form with the 250S and the 250MM. As a 3-litre, the Colombo V12 kept the 58.8mm stroke that had been established in the 166 in 1948 and went to the 73.0mm bore that would serve it until the mid-1960s. The version which helped turn the 250 Europa into the 250GT Europa was a less extreme version of the 250MM engine, with three twin-choke Weber carburettors and a quoted maximum of 220bhp. Being almost eight inches shorter than the Lampredi 3-litre, it allowed the wheelbase to be reduced to 102.4 inches. That was again an almost eight-inch reduction, which gave the otherwise unchanged shape a more purposeful proportion without compromising interior space and gave the handling a new nimbleness and balance which made the 250GT Europa a much more versatile 'dual-purpose' car than the original 250 had been.

The engine was mounted, in unit with its four-speed syncromesh gearbox (an obvious concession to road use compared to the traditional five-speed 'crash' 'box), in a chassis which apart from being short also had several other new and progressive features. Where Ferrari had used the single lower transverse leaf spring at the front, he now adopted more modern coils, and although the non-independent live rear axle sat on its usual semi-elliptic leaf springs, at least the chassis members now ran over rather than under the rear axle.

Mainly because of the cars' very active and varied competition career, those mechanical specifications were subject to constant minor revision, but this model also introduced a new kind of continuity.

Around three dozen cars were made in the first 250GT Europa series, all but one of them coupés by Pinin Farina, while the odd one out was a special coupé built by Vignale for a member of the Belgian royal family. What made the first 250GTs more of a genuine production car than anything Ferrari had made before was not so much their numbers, which were still clearly very small even by specialist manufacturer standards, but their newfound uniformity. Where virtually all his earlier cars had been made essentially to individual order, with appropriately catholic variation in both mechanical specification and styling, the majority of the 250GT Europas were far more standardised, or at least as standardised as hand building and customers with an interest in racing allowed.

That said, even that first short series, aside from the one-off Vignale car, did include a group of around nine 'special-bodied' cars by Pinin Farina. Four of them were produced essentially as competition coupés, bridging the gap between the 250MM and the first of the series-production competition 250GT berlinettas which came to be known as the Tour de France models. The first Pinin Farina competition 250GTs themselves accumulated an impressive racing record both in Europe and the USA, and Ferrari was now exploiting his successes more diligently. A couple of this 'competition' series also doubled up as Pinin Farina show cars, one of them being shown in Paris in 1955 with

pronounced Cadillac-style tail fins and considerably more chrome draped across the front, and another was shown at the 1956 Geneva Show, taking that theme and toning it down slightly to produce what turned out to be a much more Americanised looking car whose influence was clear in the next series of 250GTs.

That next stop was the Boano/Ellena 250GT line, which was a direct successor to the original, and obviously drew on the look of the aforementioned show cars in the first series. Pinin Farina had started work on the new design in 1955, the intention being to extend the successful system of Ferrari building the chassis and Pinin Farina adding standardised coachwork, but Farina's success had temporarily brought a problem of its own; the company was building a new, much larger production facility, but until it was complete they wouldn't have the space to build Ferraris in the numbers now required. The solution was to farm the work out to another house, Carrozzeria Boano, whose founder Mario Boano had worked for both Stabilimenti Farina and Pinin Farina.

The new car, introduced in Paris in 1956, was almost pure 250GT Europa under the skin, with modest updating. Boano built around eighty cars and then went to head Fiat's styling department, leaving his son-in-law, Ezio Ellena, to take over the Carrozzeria and build the cars under his own name from 1958, with further styling and minor mechanical changes. Ellena built another fifty 250GTs, and with them finally established the model's position as a true production Ferrari with a gleaming future.

Both the large, oval, 'egg-crate' grille (top) and the Borrani centre-lock wire wheels (above) were Ferrari trademarks on cars of this period, the wheels offering strength with lightness and the grille ample cooling for the steadily larger V12s.

Under the bonnet (right, above) the shorter Colombo V12 helped create ample interior space even on the shorter wheelbase; under the tail (right) the big main chassis members now ran over rather than under the still leaf-sprung rear axle.

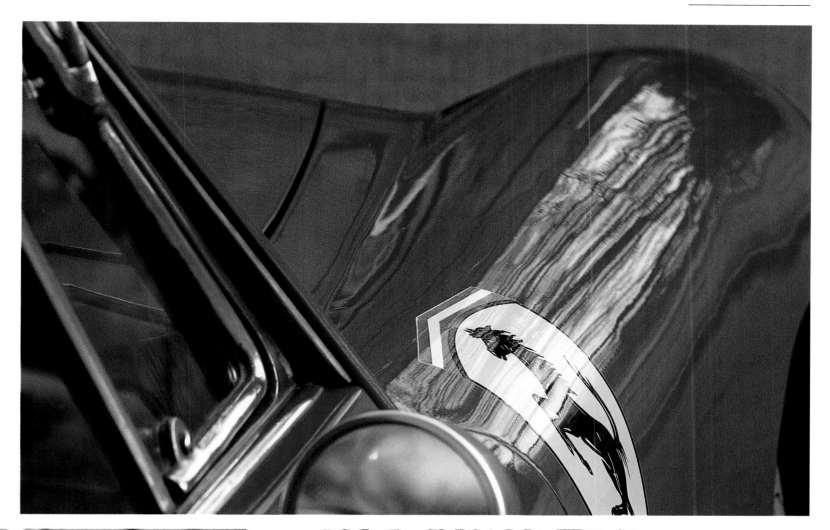

250GT EUROPA
SPECIFICATION

ENGINE
60° V12

CAPACITY
2953cc

BORE x STROKE
73.0 x 58.8mm

COMPRESSION RATIO
9.0:1

POWER
220bhp

VALVE GEAR
Single overhead camshafts

FUEL SYSTEM
Three Weber 36DCF
carburettors

TRANSMISSION
Four-speed manual

FRONT SUSPENSION
Independent, by double
wishbones, transverse leaf
spring, lever dampers

REAR SUSPENSION
Non-independent, by live axle,
semi-elliptic leaf springs, parallel
arms, lever dampers

BRAKES
All drums

WHEELS
Centre-lock wire

WEIGHT
c.2500lb (1134kg)

MAXIMUM SPEED
c.130mph (209kph)

NUMBER MADE, DATES
c.36, 1954–5

250GT
CABRIOLET

Perhaps the biggest surprise about Ferrari's first series-built cabriolet was that Ferrari took so long to get round to it; after all, one of the things that many people think really makes a sports car a sports car is an open top.

This first production Cabriolet was not, of course, the first open-topped car that Ferrari had built. Many of the early sports racers were naturally open-topped, albeit with no additional weather equipment, and there had been a handful of more civilised, touring-oriented variants of earlier road cars, but nothing built in any quantity.

The real basis for the new Pinin Farina Cabriolet was the remarkable success of the 250GT family. By 1956, there were the 250GT coupés designed for touring and the 250GT berlinettas designed for a versatile life as road or race cars. The cabrio was a natural way to extend the range and thus expand the market potential, yet Ferrari seemed more inclined to drift cautiously into the cabrio market than to make a proper once and for all effort while the coachbuilders were content to play themselves in to the new style, with what they usually called show cars but which might just as easily be regarded as prototypes.

The *very* first 250 Cabriolet, bodied by Pinin Farina and originally seen in 1953, wasn't really part of what became the successful production series at all. Popularly known as the 'Ariowitch' cabriolet after the name of its first owner, it was a 250, true enough, but it was based on one of the short run of Lampredi-engined 250 Europas, as opposed to the 'second-series' Colombo-engined 250GT Europas that were the real starting point for the 250 success story.

That 1953 car apparently didn't inspire any immediate thoughts of going into full-scale production with a cabriolet, because when the first 250GT Europa series came along, with about thirty six cars eventually built through 1954 and 1955, not one was bodied as a cabrio. Only when the next series of 250GT coupés (the Pinin Farina styled, Boana/Ellena built cars) was underway, from 1956 to 1958, did any of the dwindling band of Ferrari coachbuilders seem interested in producing a proper soft-topped Ferrari.

Mario Boano did it first, with a car for the 1956 Geneva Show. Virtually unmodified Boano coupé under the skin, it was a handsome and distinctive car, with pronounced rear fins and neat detailing.

A year later, at Geneva in 1957, it was followed by a Pinin Farina cabrio on the same 250GT basics, but with a more heavily stylised, sporty look. The long nose had

Mechanically, the 250GT Cabriolets were virtually standardised, but details like badges and vents (above and top) varied markedly.

Coupé lines are evident in the overall look of the second series Cabriolet (right), making it more a tourer than a racer.

vertical bumper bars, flanking a big grille complete with driving lights, while the tail had a massive horizontal bumper. The lights were similar to the 1956 Boano show car's, set into the upper line of the wings. The most gimmicky touch of all, though, was a deeply cut-down left door, vintage-style, ostensibly for the driver's elbow.

The show car was extensively used by Ferrari Grand Prix driver Peter Collins, who had it converted to Dunlop disc brakes – making it the first Ferrari ever to use discs. Ferrari later cannibalised them from this car to use on a racing Testa Rossa, found that they worked and soon adopted them for both production and racing.

Pinin Farina then did an even more extreme show car which he called the *'Spyder Competizione'*, with a small wraparound racing windscreen, a faired headrest for the

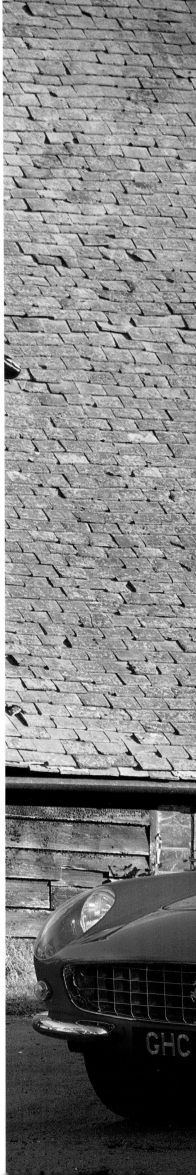

Several features distinguish the 250GT Cabriolet (right) from the apparently similar 250GT California Spyder, but the most reliable are the more upright windshield with quarter lights, and the generally more touring-oriented feel (above).

driver and a metal tonneau cover over the passenger seat area. That was another one-off, first wheeled out in public around June 1957. After another pair of progressively more conservative specials, the first series of around thirty-six production 250GT Cabriolets followed between July 1957 and July 1959.

Notwithstanding the racing connotations of the *'Spyder Competizione'*, the steel-bodied production cars had no racing pretensions; they were strictly meant as touring cars. Styling variations apart, mechanically they were virtually standardised, which was really the secret of all the 250s. Like the show cars cum prototypes, they were pure 250GT coupé under the skin, with the usual independent front, non-independent rear suspensions on a tubular ladder chassis, and the appropriate Colombo-type engine. During 1958 they changed to a horizontal front bumper, recessed driving lights, and later to conventional, unfaired headlights and they looked quietly pretty.

They were the link to the second series of 250GT Cabriolets, introduced in Paris late in 1959 to run alongside the recently introduced 250GT California Spyder. These two open-topped Ferraris were to have quite different characters and the styling changes for the second series Cabriolet were largely aimed at emphasising that.

Where the 'dual-purpose' California Spyder was recognisably related to the competition berlinettas, the Cabriolet, while retaining the feel of the first series, was given the look of the touring-oriented 250GT Pininfarina coupé

The production rear lights (above left) were rather more conventional than the prototypes', the big chromed side vents (above) only appeared on a few cars, and the badges (left) signified the model was both styled and built by Pininfarina.

which supplied all its mechanical elements.

Those now included the latest V12 with outside-plug, coil valve spring, 12-port cylinder heads, a four-speed-plus-overdrive gearbox, and disc brakes, but this generation still used the old style lever dampers.

This was a very attractive and practical Ferrari, although it was still strictly a two-seater. With its quite upright windscreen (now with separate quarter lights where the earlier car had had a 'wraparound' windscreen) it offered adequate headroom with the top erected, and a fine feeling of interior space. It was fully trimmed, well equipped and with ample soundproofing for its touring role; with its long tail it even offered plenty of usable luggage volume for two, and not long after its launch, Ferrari offered a detachable

hardtop which further improved its practicality.

It was the most expensive car in the 250GT range, and it was rather slow into production, which didn't start properly until 1960, but from there there was no looking back. In fact it would also be reasonable to interpret the fact that Ferrari sold around 200 examples of the second series Cabriolet, compared to less than forty of the first series, as a sign of a very positively growing market, but strangely, when the second series 250GT Pininfarina Cabriolet went out of production late in 1962, it wasn't immediately replaced by a car of similar character. The next generation of soft-topped touring Ferraris didn't arrive until the 275GTS was launched almost exactly two years later, towards the end of 1964. It was, of course, a major success.

The faired headlights that appeared on a few 250GT Cabriolets helped confuse them even more with their cousins the Californians, but conversely, a proportion of Caifornians had normal, exposed headlights so even they weren't a sure sign.

250GT CABRIOLET SPECIFICATION

ENGINE
60° V12

CAPACITY
2953cc

BORE x STROKE
73.0 x 58.8mm

COMPRESSION RATIO
9.0:1

POWER
240bhp

VALVE GEAR
Single overhead camshafts

FUEL SYSTEM
Three Weber 36DCF carburettors

TRANSMISSION
Four-speed manual, plus overdrive

FRONT SUSPENSION
Independent, by double wishbones, coil springs, telescopic dampers

REAR SUSPENSION
Non-independent, by live axle, semi-elliptic leaf springs, parallel arms, telescopic dampers

BRAKES
All discs

WHEELS
Centre-lock wire

WEIGHT
c.3200lb (1451kg)

MAXIMUM SPEED
c.120mph (193kph)

NUMBER MADE, DATES
c.200, 1959–62

250GTE
(250GT 2+2)

In the beginning, Enzo Ferrari built racing cars; then he sold racing cars. Next he sold racing cars that could be used on the road; then he sold road cars that could go racing. Finally he sold road cars. That was how the Ferrari market built up chronologically, it was also Enzo Ferrari's order of priorities. Throughout his life, he remained interested in the road cars almost solely as the means to the racing end.

It helps explain how the legend grew so quickly. The first Ferraris that appeared on the road were as near as made little difference to the Ferraris that were concurrently winning on the track, and that got them noticed. By the early 1950s, a Ferrari was already among the great motoring status symbols; racing drivers bought Ferraris to win, the smart set increasingly bought Ferraris to be seen in. And however skilfully he projected his disinterest, Ferrari couldn't help but sell them whatever they wanted.

With the 250GT family, he refined that to a fine art. He sold racing cars, race-cum-road cars, road-cum-race cars and pure road cars; he sold berlinettas and spyders, coupés and cabriolets, with all the style and performance that anyone could ask for.

Or almost anyone. With the multiplicity of 250s, Ferrari had matured by the end of the 1950s from a maker of one-offs to a genuine series producer. His special and highly successful relationship with Pininfarina, as engineer and stylist respectively, had combined with the popularity and versatility of the 250s to change the whole nature of the business. Ferraris were no longer 'bespoke' cars for which Ferrari supplied only the chassis, leaving the customer to make his own choice from the coachwork catalogue like choosing wallpaper or furniture fabric. Ferrari did still supply only the chassis, but in almost every case now, Pininfarina clothed them to something closer to an 'off-the-peg' uniformity. It made the numbers involved change dramatically, until Ferrari was no longer selling cars by the dozen but by the hundred.

While Ferrari was growing up, his clientele were growing up too. By the late 1950s, the man (or woman) who had bought a no-compromise Ferrari in the late 1940s might well have a young family to complicate his (or her) love of cars, but to date, Ferrari, for all his berlinettas and spyders, coupés and cabriolets couldn't really cater for that scenario; the one thing that he *didn't* have was a 2+2. Some of his rivals did, though, and that only made the situation worse.

The 250GTE might have had four seats but there was nothing to say it wasn't intended as a proper sporty car for enthusiastic owners, as the usual Borrani wire wheels (left) and the additional driving lights (far right) go to show.

Ferrari and Pininfarina set to work early in 1959 to solve the problem together, within certain parameters. The new car might have four seats but it still had to be a Ferrari. There *had* been Ferraris with more than two seats before, but both the seats and the production had been little more than token gestures, with cars made in tiny numbers as parts of already short runs, such as the 212 Inter or the 342 America. What Ferrari now wanted was a genuine large-series production 2+2, still with the Ferrari mystique.

It would be based, of course, on the ubiquitous 250GT underpinnings, and it would be as compact and sporting as possible. Ferrari decreed that the wheelbase would not be allowed to grow beyond the 102.4 inches of the longer-wheelbase 250 berlinettas, which presented Pininfarina with an interesting problem in packaging the long V12 engine and up to four people. Ferrari and Pininfarina met these seemingly impossible aims very convincingly.

The key was to reposition the engine within an otherwise largely unchanged chassis, moving it forwards by some eight inches to liberate space for a bigger cockpit, which allowed the new rear seats to be fitted in ahead of the rear axle line. The tracks at front and rear were made minimally wider, but otherwise the chassis dimensions stayed the same. The car itself was about a foot longer overall than the two-seater berlinetta. There was marginally more overhang at the front, thanks to the engine and radiator needing more forward space, but most of the added length was in the tail, where the 2+2 was given rather more generous luggage space than most Ferraris. During 1959, Ferrari and Pininfarina built a small number of prototypes of their 2+2. From the start, the basic shape was virtually finalised, but there were several detail differences between versions,

Ferrari and Pininfarina did a fine job on their first serious 2+2 (overleaf). Moving the engine well forward in an unchanged wheelbase left scope for reasonable cabin space, and also allowed the feel of a coupé rather than a saloon.

notably around the headlights, cooling and ventilation vents and the exhaust trims.

It was with one of the prototypes that Ferrari introduced the 250GT 2+2 to the public. For a change, the first appearance wasn't at a motor show but at a motor race, as Ferrari supplied one of the three prototypes to be used as an official course car at Le Mans in June 1960. Not surprisingly, it generated a great deal of interest. For one thing, a genuine 2+2 really did represent a big step for Ferrari; for another it had the element of surprise, having been one of Maranello's better-kept secrets through the prototype stages. Neither did it do the new car's image any harm when six of the first seven places in the 24-Hours were taken by one derivative after another of the 250 family, led home by Paul Frère and Olivier Gendebien in a 250 Testa Rossa.

The new car, known as either the 250GT 2+2 or 250GTE, appeared in production form for the first time in October 1960, at Ferrari's favourite launch venue, the Paris Show. It was powered by a 240bhp, three-carburettor version of the 3-litre V12, lifted more or less directly from the two-seater 250GTs, with Testa Rossa-type cylinder heads using coil rather than the old hairpin type valve springs, separate inlet ports and with the spark plugs on the outside of the heads. The chassis was also little changed from the normal 250GT layout, with independent front suspension by wishbones and coil springs and non-independent rear suspension for the live axle by leaf springs and parallel trailing arms. In common with the two-seater coupés, it adopted telescopic dampers and disc brakes.

It was a major success in almost every respect. It did provide adequate accommodation in the rear for two average sized people over reasonable distances, or quite generous space for the two children who were the most likely occupants. It was luxuriously trimmed, of course, and extremely comfortable.

Pininfarina had achieved a look that was far more coupé than saloon, beautifully balanced in spite of its size, and free of any ostentation save a simple styling line along the flanks, just above the wheelarches, to tone down the large, flat side panels. He had built in just about adequate roof height for adult rear seat passengers but disguised it by the graceful sweep of the side window line and the dramatic slope of both rear window and tail.

It went like a Ferrari too. It was considerably heavier than the two-seaters, of course, but it was an ideal fast tourer. If it had any dynamic fault it was that moving the engine forward had increased its tendency to understeer when cornering hard, but that wasn't the sort of driving it was usually destined for.

It went through three series and sold in far greater numbers that anyone had probably envisaged – 229 in the first series, 356 in the second (introduced in 1962 with minor interior changes) and another 300 in the third (in 1963, with chrome headlight rims, driving lights moved to outside the grille, and revised tail lights). Late in 1963, a few cars were built with the new 4-litre 330 engine in the 250GT 2+2 chassis, and they provided the logical bridge to the 330GT 2+2, as introduced in January 1964.

The **GTE** sensibly didn't skimp on interior luxuries (far left), yet had enough exterior styling clues (left, above and below) to leave absolutely no doubt that it was a true Ferrari.

250GTE (250GT 2+2) SPECIFICATION

ENGINE
60° V12

CAPACITY
2953cc

BORE x STROKE
73.0 × 58.8mm

COMPRESSION RATIO
8.8:1

POWER
240bhp

VALVE GEAR
Single overhead camshafts

FUEL SYSTEM
Three Weber 40DCL6 carburettors

TRANSMISSION
Four-speed manual, plus overdrive

FRONT SUSPENSION
Independent, by double wishbones, coil springs, telescopic dampers

REAR SUSPENSION
Non-independent, by live axle, semi-elliptic leaf springs, parallel arms, telescopic dampers

BRAKES
All discs

WHEELS
Centre-lock wire

WEIGHT
c.3500lb (1587kg)

MAXIMUM SPEED
c.135mph (217kph)

NUMBER MADE, DATES
c.955 (in three series), 1960–63

250GT
SWB

When Pierre Levegh was killed in the world's worst ever motor racing tragedy, at Le Mans in 1955, the accident not only cost the lives of over eighty spectators too, but also gave the sport's governing body cause seriously to rethink the way sports car racing was going. Not for the first time, and not for the last, they concluded that the cars of the day were getting to be too fast and too dangerous.

Mindful of the fact that another disaster like Le Mans might destroy motor sport forever, they took the brave decision in 1956 to try and tone down the most extreme form of sports racers (many of them little more than two-seater Grand Prix cars) and promote the notion of production-based cars. So in addition to requiring that the out-and-out sports racers should have two doors, a full-width windscreen and nominal provision for a hood, the FIA also placed a lot more importance on GT cars; cars that in theory at least could be driven to the circuit, raced competitively and driven home again.

For Ferrari, building such dual-purpose cars presented few problems. It was after all something he had done to a greater or lesser extent ever since he came into the car building business back in 1947, and having GTs as a more

prestigious international racing category could only be good news commercially; providing, of course, that Ferraris were winning.

He already had the basic elements, in the guise of the long-wheelbase 250GT berlinettas, which in turn had evolved from the 250GT Europa. That Europa, introduced in 1954, was the first car that Ferrari had officially called a GT, and it had the Colombo engine where the earlier 250 Europa had had a Lampredi V12. The 250GT Europas (and the 'Boana/Ellena' 250 coupés which followed) were principally meant as civilised road cars; the 250GT Berlinettas, introduced in 1956, were really customer competition cars. They were homologated mainly on the strength of those mechanically similar contemporaneous coupés, but had quite different aluminium bodies with all the usual weight-saving tricks such as perspex rear and side windows and minimal trim. In September 1956, one of the Berlinettas won the gruelling Tour de France and thereafter that was how the Berlinettas were always popularly known – as the 250GT Tour de France.

If any kind of illustration were needed of Ferrari's pre-eminence in GT racing, his record in the Tour de France is it. The event was a mixture of races and rallying, stretched

Details like the almost complete lack of external trim (below) and huge quick-action filler cap (right) show the 250GT SWB's main purpose as a racing model, but one surprisingly at home on the road too. B 400 (overleaf) is one of the most famous of all SWBs . . .

over several thousand miles and many days of competition, with road sections between events, very harsh schedules to meet and minimal servicing allowed. Ferrari won it in 1951, were second in 1952 and 1953, and won again every year from 1956 to 1961.

The 'Tour de France' Berlinettas were very typical of Ferrari's customer competition cars in the way their specification varied virtually from car to car, with any number of styling variations and a broad sweep of engine development. Then, early in 1959, a more radical variant appeared with a much rounder, lower-nosed body shape, yet still on the usual Tour de France chassis.

Ferrari built seven of this model in all. Mechanically, it was almost identical to any other Berlinetta, its principal purpose, with hindsight, obviously being to test the new and hopefully more aerodynamic body shape. To that end, he sent two of them to Le Mans in 1959 where they ran quite well but were beaten by a conventional Tour de France, which finished third overall and duly won the GT category.

Ferrari wouldn't have been too disappointed; the logical conclusion of the move that had started with what retrospectively became known as the 'interim' 250GT Berlinetta

appeared at the Paris Salon in October 1959. Styled by Pininfarina and built by Scaglietti, it looked virtually identical to the interim car but had lost the small fixed rear quarter windows. That was because it had also lost 7.9 inches (200mm) out of the wheelbase, to become not only a more aerodynamic car than the old Tour de France but also a rather lighter and more compact one, with appropriately better performance and nimbler handling. It became known as the 250GT Short-Wheelbase Berlinetta, or 250GT SWB.

The new proportions suited it beautifully and it was a stunningly purposeful looking car. The short, square nose with its large, deep grille actually turned out to be a bit bluff for really effective aerodynamics, but it gave the new model a very aggressive visage. Many details changed over the years, but the basic shape never did. And there was a lot more to the new model than just the new look and the short wheelbase. The new chassis, although broadly similar to the Tour de France's typical Ferrari ladder, had some additional stiffening, and two specific leaps forward – from drum brakes to Dunlop discs all round, and from the old lever-type dampers to modern telescopics.

Of course, the SWB's short-stroke 2953cc Colombo V12

. . . its dark blue colours and white nose stripe are the livery of Rob Walker, who ran chassis number 2735 for Stirling Moss – to win both the British Empire Trophy and the Tourist Trophy in 1961, as part of a very distinguished career.

68

For a while, B 400 wore a lightweight shell designed by Bizzarrini and built by Drogo, but after a racing accident in 1967 and some years of neglect it has been restored to its original Scaglietti-bodied glory (above), with the correct trim (left) to make it a perfectly bearable road car.

250GT SWB SPECIFICATION

ENGINE
60° V12

CAPACITY
2953cc

BORE x STROKE
73.0 x 58.8mm

COMPRESSION RATIO
9.7:1

POWER
280bhp

VALVE GEAR
Single overhead camshafts

FUEL SYSTEM
Three Weber 40DCL6 carburettors

TRANSMISSION
Four-speed manual, plus overdrive

FRONT SUSPENSION
Independent, by double wishbones, coil springs, telescopic dampers

REAR SUSPENSION
Non-independent, by live axle, semi-elliptic leaf springs, parallel arms, telescopic dampers

BRAKES
All discs

WHEELS
Centre-lock wire

WEIGHT
c.2500lb (1134kg)

MAXIMUM SPEED
c.155mph (249kph)

NUMBER MADE, DATES
c.165, 1959–62

was derived from the Tour de France too, but again with some significant changes, notably around the cylinder heads which adopted conventional coil valve springs, 12-port induction, more studs for better gas sealing and re-sited plugs for better combustion and racing accessibility. Road cars had up to 240bhp on three Webers, competition versions were typically quoted as giving 280bhp.

Ferrari launched the 250GT SWB as a competition GT and an even hotter successor to the ultra-successful Tour de France, but even when he launched it he promised a softer variant to run alongside the basic model; a Lusso, in effect, which would still be aimed at GT racing in the true sense of word, while being even more daily usable as a road car. It would have a mainly steel body (with aluminium doors, boot and bonnet) where the dedicated competition car used largely aluminium, glass where there was plastic, front quarter bumpers and a full rear bumper, more interior trim, milder engine tune and softer suspension. Or any permutation thereof. There might even be luggage space thanks to a smaller fuel tank that didn't totally fill the boot.

Interestingly, of the 163 250GT SWBs that Ferrari built, seventy-four were designated as competition cars and eighty-nine as road cars; in 1959 the two that were built

were both racers, in 1960 the racers still outnumbered the Lussos three to one in a total production of sixty, in the SWB's biggest year, 1961, the road cars had taken over with forty-one of the total of sixty-six cars built, and in 1962 just two of the final run of thirty-five were specifically racers. Of the 1961 cars, twenty-two were to a particularly high spec and became popularly known as the 'SEFAC hot-rods', SEFAC being the acronym for Ferrari's full company name. These cars gave close to 300bhp and helped Ferrari to another convincing GT title in 1961.

The model was a prolific race winner for many years, scoring huge numbers of outright as well as class wins at all levels. Yet most of all, after all these years, the 250GT SWB is still widely regarded as the ultimate *dual-purpose* Ferrari, the one that, more than any other, a customer really could drive to the track, race, and drive home. Ferrari built other cars before and after that could do the same thing, but none with such an impeccable balance between the two roles. It was really less of a specialised racer than either the Tour de France that preceded it or the magnificent 250GTO that followed, but few Ferraris have ever given so many people so much success and so much practical pleasure all in the same package.

250GTO

Legend is an over-used word in the glossary of classic motor cars, but legends don't come much bigger than the car which Enzo Ferrari used to steamroller his way to the world championships for GT cars in 1962, 1963 and 1964. It wasn't quite the last front-engined car to win the major title for sports and GT cars; Carroll Shelby's Cobra-based Daytona coupé did that in 1965, but thereafter science increasingly displaced brute force in top-level sports car racing as mid-engined cars like Ford's GT40 and Ferrari's own LMs, Ss and Ps took over. Nowadays, they are all held in a degree of awe and reverence but none more so than the mighty 250GTO.

It was a car with an air of destiny, the perfect embodiment of everything Ferrari held dearest. It was a racing car without compromise, that not only *could* be usable on the road, but by the regulations which created it, *had* to be usable on the road. As the 1950s gave way to the 1960s, Ferrari was already deeply committed to GT racing, which had been an international racing category with its own championship since 1956. In 1961, the FIA announced that for 1962 the GT championship would in effect be the World Championship for Sports Cars. Ferrari, having dominated the GT championships since their inception, with various derivatives of his 250GT, was delighted and he attacked the problem with a vengeance.

This was grist to the Ferrari mill. The cars for the new GT championship needed to be road legal and built in sufficient numbers to satisfy the FIA's homologation requirements. That meant a minimum of 100 cars. To a layman, that might sound clear enough; to a skilled interpreter of the rules like Ferrari it was no more than a fairly flexible definition of his target.

He already had his starting point in the highly successful 250GT SWB. That was a very up-to-date platform, barely a couple of years old when Ferrari became aware of the new status for GTs, and by then he had already started on the next generation.

The period was an important, transitional one for racing. Grand Prix cars had gone mid-engined and found the benefits stretched to aerodynamics as well as to chassis balance. Sports cars still had a few years to go before their mid-engined revolution, but the aerodynamic argument was becoming more and more persuasive as the cars grew faster. The physical law governing the relationship between power and speed is one of rapidly diminishing returns; the

faster you go, the faster the power needed grows, and the last few mph that make the difference between a winner and an also-ran are the ones that take the most power of all.

Carroll Shelby recognised that after Ferrari had given the lead, but his example is a perfect illustration. His Cobras, even the early small-engined ones, were virtually uncatchable on shorter circuits because their prodigious power to weight ratio gave them a race-winning edge out of corners and on relatively short straights. On the long straights typical of the kind of circuit used for world class sports car racing, however, they were almost literally stopped in their tracks by being little more aerodynamic than a small building; for all their power, they just weren't fast enough on a long circuit. Morever, Shelby soon found that even the fearsome power of the big-engined Cobra made little difference to maximum speed; what was required was science. Shelby found the answer with the Daytona coupé, but by then the 250GTO had been winning for two years.

For Ferrari, it was a turning point. He was first and foremost an engine man, content that, all else being equal, he would always have the power to beat all-comers. Aerodynamics moved the goalposts, and Ferrari had to move with the times. The 250GT SWB had been a step in the right direction, but it had a nasty tendency to lift its nose at very high speeds and Ferrari knew that the speeds in the new category would be higher than ever. He knew too, however, that the SWB had to be his starting point for the new car because that was the only way he could meet the

With the mighty GTO, Ferrari discovered a new science to add to his obsession with engine power, the science of aerodynamics. From its low nose (right) with minimal cooling drag to its cut-off Kamm-type tail, the GTO was as slippery as could be.

In profile (overleaf), the 1963 GTO shows the extreme lowness of the car below the waistline, the original, fastback roofline, and the tall 'ducktail' spoiler topping the Kamm tail, to improve stability at very high straightline speeds.

homologation requirements. In effect, he was using a loophole; the FIA said 100 cars, but they also allowed for the evolution of an existing car which already satisfied the requirements. To the FIA that meant minor modifications to the bodywork; to Ferrari it meant virtually carte blanche.

At Le Mans in 1961, Ferrari ran a SWB with bodywork derived from the sleek 400 Superamerica and although the car didn't finish it showed promise. Early in 1962, it finished fourth in a three-hour race at Daytona.

More work had already been done on the new car by Giotto Bizzarrini. Bizzarrini had joined Alfa in 1954 as a chassis test engineer, and moved to Ferrari in 1957 as engine designer, chassis engineer and aerodynamicist. He is widely regarded as the father of the GTO. Having gained his engineering degree from the University of Pisa in 1953, and still working occasionally as a visiting lecturer, he had access to their wind tunnel and made the most of it before he left Ferrari in the infamous mass defection of November 1961. By then the GTO was pretty well finalised.

The slippery and beautiful new shape (built by Scaglietti) with its lower nose and abruptly-chopped Kamm tail, clothed what was ostensibly a 250GT SWB chassis; the additional small tubular structures which made it something nearer a space frame were only there to support the new bodywork, of course. Ferrari did have the decency to retain the live rear axle layout, albeit with considerable revision, including a Watts linkage.

Power, some 300bhp of it, came from the dry-sumped 3-litre six-carburettor Testa Rossa engine, a full-race unit built in the lightest possible materials, which was at least homologated for the 250s. The engine was set further back in the chassis, mounted lower down and mated to a new five-speed gearbox, all of which was accepted as evolution.

There were no bumpers, virtually no interior trim, plastic in all the windows save the windscreen and not even a speedometer, but the car now fulfilled (if only barely) the FIA's requirement that it be road usable. Now Ferrari should, by the letter of the rules, have built 100 of them. He didn't, probably couldn't have, and almost certainly never had any intentions to; for one thing he didn't feel that many people could even have handled the new model. Instead he argued that the new car, in his interpretation of the regulations, was simply an extension of the already homologated 250GT SWB series. He refused to budge, the FIA gave in and the GT (officially just a competition 250GT Berlinetta) gained an 'O' for *omologato*, to become, in popular parlance, the legendary 250GTO. Ferrari showed it off at his annual racing team press conference in February 1962 and by the end of the year it had won the first of its three successive championships. In the end he built just thirty-nine examples, including three with 4-litre engines and three final cars in 1964 with a wider, lower body, on new wider wheels and tyres.

Remarkably, the GTO in small doses *is* usable on the road, as reliable and good to drive as to look at. Now one of the most valuable and sought-after Ferraris of all, its passing from top-class competition driving was the glorious end of an era.

One lesson that Ferrari (and Bizzarrini) learned with the 250GT SWB and GTO proto-types was that a long, low nose (left) was vital for low drag with good resistance to lift. U-shaped covers mask additional cooling vents, and straps retain bonnet.

250GTO SPECIFICATION

ENGINE
60° V12

CAPACITY
2953cc

BORE x STROKE
73.0 x 58.8mm

COMPRESSION RATIO
9.8:1

POWER
280bhp

VALVE GEAR
Single overhead camshafts

FUEL SYSTEM
Six Weber 36DCN carburettors

TRANSMISSION
Five-speed manual

FRONT SUSPENSION
Independent, by double wishbones, coil springs, telescopic dampers

REAR SUSPENSION
Non-independent, by live axle, semi-elliptic leaf springs, parallel arms, telescopic dampers

BRAKES
All discs

WHEELS
Centre-lock wire

WEIGHT
c.2400lb (1088kg)

MAXIMUM SPEED
c.175mph (281kph)

NUMBER MADE, DATES
39, 1962–4

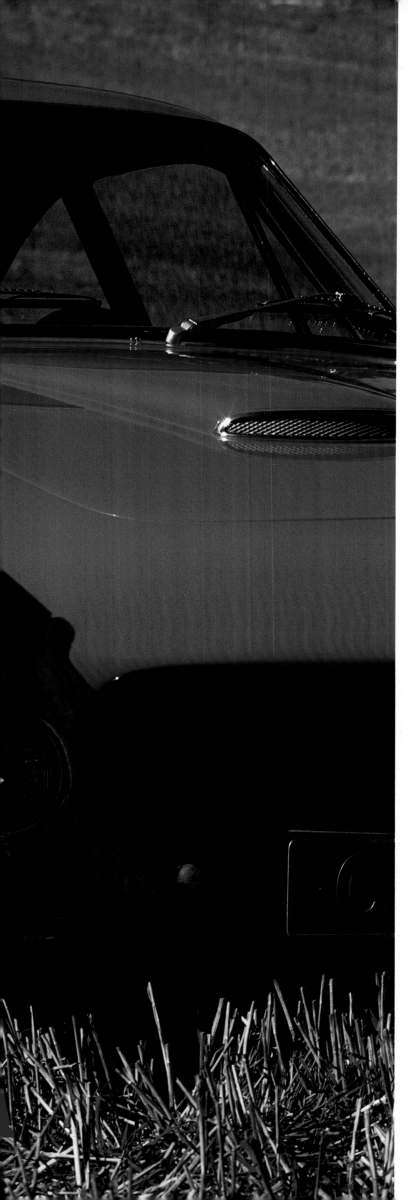

250GT BERLINETTA LUSSO

The 250GT Berlinetta Lusso wasn't around for long by Ferrari road car standards (for just about 18 months in fact, between early 1963 and mid-1964, with exactly 350 examples built), but it proved to be both a significant car and one regarded with enormous affection by Ferrari cognoscenti. Certainly many of the latter would argue, for instance, that the Berlinetta Lusso is well up there amongst the prettiest of all Ferraris, but it has to be recorded too as the last flowering of the long-running 250 dynasty (which had been Ferrari's staple roadgoing product for over a decade) and the first seed of a new generation.

It was first shown in prototype form, as styled by Pininfarina, at the 1962 Paris Motor Show, and although it wasn't quite ready when the show's doors opened, it was wheeled onto the stand shortly before the show closed. It was already rather more than just a show car, it was virtually ready for production, and once Scaglietti (who were to build it) had made some very minor practical changes, it was ready to go.

Although it was strictly a two-seater, it wasn't quite a simple successor to the last of the 250GT coupé line. It incorporated some of the softer and more luxurious philosophy of the bigger 250GT 2+2 too, spiced with overtones of the 250GT short-wheelbase berlinetta and 250GTO racing models in its elegant body shape. In other words, it hinted at the racing heritage aesthetically while opening an ever-widening gap mechanically between the real competition cars and the newer generation of Ferrari road cars.

It was a vital change; at one and the same time, motor racing was becoming ever more specialised while road car customers were becoming ever more sophisticated and demanding. While Ingegnere Ferrari could still support the outward impression of building his road cars only to support his beloved racing team, even he had grudgingly to accept commercial reality by the early 1960s.

The clues to the new thinking in the Lusso were plentiful; for a start, the name itself translates literally as 'luxury', but more than that, the whole layout and structure of the car had moved significantly away from the no-compromise ethic of the street-racer days and towards a bit more space and comfort.

There was plenty of Ferrari thoroughbred thinking at base, of course, but it was softened. The 3-litre Colombo V12 was closely similar to that in the recent 250GT SWB – a true dual-purpose road and track machine. By Ferrari

In the Berlinetta Lusso (left), Pininfarina styled one of the most beautiful of all Ferraris. The nose and tail treatments echo the competition-bred 250GT SWB and 250GTO respectively, but new chassis proportions gave it a look all its own.

From any angle, the Lusso has a sculptural beauty, and in spite of its apparent cabin size, Ferrari kept it strictly as a spacious two-seater rather than a 2+2.

standards, though, this version was quite a mild engine, with the usual chain-driven single overhead camshaft per bank and two valves per cylinder, but just three twin-choke downdraught Webers where the racing engines invariably had six. At best it was reckoned good for 250bhp at 7500rpm, and perhaps 206lb ft of torque at 5500 – good figures but certainly no better than the best of the earlier roadgoing 250s.

The change of direction was perhaps most evident, though, in the disposition of the engine in the chassis. The chassis itself was a tubular ladder based on that of the 250GTO (in turn evolved from those of the short-wheelbase 250GT berlinettas). It had the familiar 94½-inch wheelbase, and the same trailing arms, Watt's linkage and semi-elliptic spring layout for the non-independent rear suspension – plus supplementary coil springs concentric with the telescopic dampers, as also seen on the GTO. The front suspension was independent, by unequal length double wishbones and coil springs, and the brakes were discs all-round, behind beautiful Borrani centre-lock wire wheels.

The big difference in layout for the Lusso was that the engine had been moved forward by several inches. It was the last thing that Ferrari would have wanted to do in a racing model, where concentrating the weight in the centre is important, but it was clearly an advantage in a pure road car, in allowing a little more uncluttered passenger space, especially in this generation when the big four-speed gearbox was still on the back of the engine, not yet in the back of the car. And, finally, the body was all in steel save for the door skins, bonnet and boot lid, and some of the internal underpinnings, the trim was generous by Ferrari standards, and the car was by no means a lightweight.

Inside, it harked back to the competition cars with its

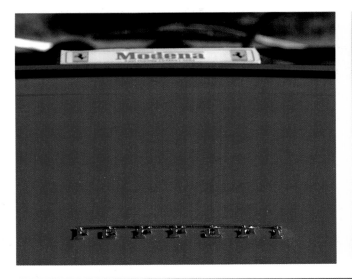

unusually deep bucket seats for a pure Ferrari road car, then contradicted the racing connection with a strange dashboard layout that was unique to this car – with the five minor instruments dead ahead in a row above the steering column, but the big 180mph (289kph) speedometer and 8000rpm tachometer right in the middle of the dash, and slightly angled towards the driver. There were other minor anomalies to the luxury tag; the reasonably generous space behind the seats was lined with quilted leather and equipped with straps to tie down some luggage (the tiny boot was virtually filled with spare wheel and tool kit) but the seat backs wouldn't tilt to give access; and although the seats wouldn't adjust for rake either, or the steering wheel for tilt

or reach, it *was* possible to adjust the pedals fore and aft by a couple of inches, which is rather more in line with racing practice, so maybe the new Lusso wasn't quite so committed to its new line of thinking after all.

And, all that said, it still had real Ferrari performance and manners, with a top speed of around 150mph (241kph), a respectable if not shattering 0–60mph (97kph) time of about 7 seconds (hampered slightly by a rather high first gear), and 0–100mph (161kph) in less than 17 seconds. Its chassis, even with the forward engine stance, was good enough to give it the legs of pretty well anything – save another Ferrari, that is.

Performance notwithstanding though, the Pininfarina

As well as in the elegant proportioning, Pininfarina made the Lusso work in its neatly understated details, even in the way he dealt with front driving lights and minimalist bumper bars (above left and top centre).

The rear of the Lusso (left) wasn't just beautifully simple, it was also very sound aerodynamically, with the smooth roofline blending into the classic cut-off of a drag-reducing Kamm-tail. The big central instruments were unique to the Lusso.

250GT BERLINETTA LUSSO
SPECIFICATION

ENGINE
60° V12

CAPACITY
2953cc

BORE x STROKE
73.0 × 58.8mm

COMPRESSION RATIO
9.2:1

POWER
250bhp

VALVE GEAR
Single overhead camshafts

FUEL SYSTEM
Three Weber DCL3 carburettors

TRANSMISSION
Four-speed manual

FRONT SUSPENSION
Independent, by double wishbones, coil springs, telescopic dampers

REAR SUSPENSION
Non-independent, by live axle, semi-elliptic leaf springs, parallel arms, telescopic dampers

BRAKES
All discs

WHEELS
Centre-lock wire

WEIGHT
c.2600lb (1179kg)

MAXIMUM SPEED
c.150mph (241kph)

NUMBER MADE, DATES
c.350, 1962–4

styling is surely the Lusso's greatest asset, highly distinctive alongside earlier members of the 250 line yet drawing subtly from several of them. It mixes a beautiful and practical lightness of line above the waist with a purposeful solidity below it, soft curves blending delicately with square-cut angles. The nose might well suggest the SWB's aggressive droop-snootiness for instance, and the tail has more than a hint of the GTO's aerodynamic purity with its abruptly chopped Kamm panel and sweeping rear deck, but the Lusso has a look all of its own.

Battista 'Pinin' Farina, head of the Pininfarina dynasty, ran a special 250GT Berlinetta Lusso himself from 1963, which suggests that he was particularly pleased with it, but

it has been said that Enzo Ferrari was never entirely comfortable with the artistic grace of the Lusso; he thought a Ferrari, even one that was supposedly distancing itself from the racing models, should have more aggression in its lines.

That, though, was at best only coincidental in the short career of the Berlinetta Lusso. The real point was that at last, after more than ten years and some 2500 cars, the 250 line itself was drawing to a close. Because whatever he might have thought of the aesthetics, Ferrari was at heart an engine man, and, late in 1964, the 250s' long-serving, 3-litre Colombo V12 was just about to grow up into a new and technically more sophisticated generation, in the first of the 3.3-litre 275s.

250GT
CALIFORNIA
SPYDER

Sleek lines of the Spyder changed very little between long-wheelbase models (left and overleaf) and the later short-wheelbase. Side vents, a narrower grille and lack of quarter windows are most reliable way to distinguish a Spyder from a Cabrio; both had faired lights (below).

When Ferrari introduced the notion of 'gran turismo' cars to his range in the mid-1950s, he opened up a whole new market. The GTs, as launched with the 250GT Europa in 1954, were a reflection of the shift in emphasis for top level sports car racing, away from purely purpose-built racers and towards something more nearly akin to what could be used on the road. Before the change, racing sports cars were becoming not unlike two-seater Grand Prix cars – very fast, very costly and, so far as the organisers were concerned, very dangerous. After the change, it was quite feasible to race a car that you would run on the road; and if the car was a Ferrari, it was perfectly possible to race it and win with it.

Of course, even Ferrari's clientele by this stage included those who had no interest whatsoever in racing their Ferraris, preferring instead to treat them purely as rapid and status-improving road cars. Ferrari catered profitably for both markets, with the berlinettas for the racers and road/racers, and the more civilised coupés for the non-combatant Ferraristi. From 1957 he also offered the rather pretty Pinin Farina cabriolets.

The cabrios were quite different in character from earlier open-topped Ferraris, in that far from being racer-clones they were much more closely related to the touring coupés, with full trim, plentiful if simple creature comforts and generally only a relatively mild state of tune. They were hugely successful, but in the usual way of the world, someone always wants more.

In this case, it was America that wanted more. One recently, America had more or less simultaneously discovered European-style motor racing and European-style sports cars. They made the discovery in the years immediately after World War 2, when lots of GIs went home from European tours of duty and took the little sports cars they had discovered and enjoyed there with them. At first, people laughed at the tiny MGs and Jaguars and the like, but when they showed how they could run rings round the typical US-built behemoths on both road and track, the laughing stopped and the sports car sales boom started. Within a few years, virtually every European sports car maker of any note was selling the vast majority of his output in America, and especially selling soft tops to the West Coast, where the sun always shines.

Ferrari was no exception; having sold his first cars in America even before the 1940s were out, by the mid-1950s

he had established a formidable racing reputation and, on the strength of that, the foundations of a large and lucrative road car market. Anything he sold in Europe, he sold in America, and beyond that he was always happy to respond when someone wanted more – providing, of course, that they were happy to pay.

The someone who wanted more in 1958 was possibly Ferrari's main importer, Luigi Chinetti, but more probably the West Coast distributor, John von Neumann. Von Neumann could already offer his discerning Ferrari fans the usual European fare of road-race berlinettas, touring coupés and touring cabrios, but he was being asked too for a cabrio that could occasionally go racing – something that the well-trimmed but heavy Pinin Farina cabrios as introduced in 1957 really weren't designed to do. So Neumann suggested a car that was more along the lines of a drophead version of the berlinettas rather than the cabrio-style drophead version of the milder coupé, and Ferrari was happy to oblige.

By December 1957 he had a prototype of what was to become known as the 250GT California Spyder. It was styled by Pininfarina, and broadly looked like the cabrio, until you looked more closely. Then you would find a smaller, more rounded grille, a less extreme windscreen

wraparound but much steeper 'screen rake, more aggressively sporty cooling vents in the front flanks, and different, more conventional rear lights. Under the skin you would have found almost precisely the same mechanical specification as on the contemporaneous 250GT 'Tour de France' berlinettas – among the first of the classic 'dual-purpose' GT Ferraris.

That meant the same 102.4-inch (2600mm) wheelbase tubular ladder chassis with independent coil and wishbone front suspension and live axle, semi-elliptic rear suspension. It meant drum brakes and lever shock absorbers, and a familiar version of the 3-litre Colombo engine, with siamesed inlet ports, hairpin valve springs, spark plugs towards the centre of the vee, and three twin-choke downdraught carburettors. According to Ferrari, that gave up to 250bhp, which was a bit more than the cabrio, and although the Spyder was inevitably heavier than the berlinetta (because chopping the top off a car always demands extra weight to replace the inherent stiffness of a closed shell) it was considerably *lighter* than the cabrio. That was partly because where the cabrio was all steel, the Spyder had aluminium doors, boot and bonnet lids, partly because Spyder buyers had to put up with more spartan trim and

Unusual clear bonnet scoop (far left) in this case covers massive single air-cleaner and three twin-choke Webers (centre, below). Full instrumentation (centre, above) keeps competition drivers happy, but trim was usually minimal. Total lack of bumpers (left) was one of several options, giving an exceptionally neat look to the shark nose – emphasising the Spyder's sporting cachet but risking vulnerability.

250GT CALIFORNIA SPYDER SPECIFICATION

ENGINE
60° V12

CAPACITY
2953cc

BORE x STROKE
73.0 x 58.8mm

COMPRESSION RATIO
9.5:1

POWER
280bhp (SWB model)

VALVE GEAR
Single overhead camshafts

FUEL SYSTEM
Three Weber 42DCL3 carburettors

TRANSMISSION
Four-speed manual

FRONT SUSPENSION
Independent, by double wishbones, coil springs, telescopic dampers

REAR SUSPENSION
Non-independent, by live axle, semi-elliptic leaf springs, parallel arms, telescopic dampers

BRAKES
All discs

WHEELS
Centre-lock wire

WEIGHT
c.2350lb (1065kg)

MAXIMUM SPEED
c.145mph (233kph)

NUMBER MADE, DATES
c.46 LWB, c.50 SWB, 1958–63

very few additional niceties – but then that was just what they had ordered.

It didn't destroy too much of the car's refinement, and it was certainly still usable on the road, but now it was a viable part-time racer too. If you did want to go racing you could order an all-aluminium body and more power. Quite a number of the forty-seven or so Spyders built in this first series did go racing, and with considerable success; Bob Grossman and Fernand Tavano, for instance, took fifth place at Le Mans in 1959, Richie Ginther and Howard Hively won the Sebring 12-Hour in 1959, and Scarlatti, Serena and Abate repeated that class win in 1960.

It was fairly obvious that the second generation California Spyder which arrived in May 1960 was taking the racing potential a step further. Ferrari had already improved the car during its initial run by substituting the improved cylinder heads with twelve inlet ports, coil valve springs and outside plugs; the clutch had been uprated and the car generally developed through racing. Now he introduced a new, short-wheelbase version, in line with the change from long to short wheelbase for the berlinettas. A short car meant less weight and better handling, and with the latest version of the 12-port, outside-plug engine it was

more powerful too, with up to 280bhp in normal trim and more with full competition options.

Not only was the chassis some eight inches (203mm) shorter at 94.5 inches (2400mm), but it was more modern, with telescopic dampers instead of the old lever type, disc brakes, and overdrive for the four-speed gearbox. It didn't look like a topless version of the new short-wheelbase berlinetta, though, more like a shorter and very slightly wider version of the original long-wheelbase California Spyder. By any standards, it was one of the most stunningly beautiful of all Ferraris, possibly spoiled a little visually on a few late cars which had exposed headlights with chrome rims in place of the usual fully covered ones.

It still didn't sell in vast numbers, probably about fifty-seven up to the end of production in February 1963, to take the total California Spyder production just past 100 cars, but it was a great success in further opening up the American market. The Sports Car Club of America had obviously noticed its progress in another direction too, and the coming of the short-wheelbase model moved the Spyder out of their GT categories for racing and into the modified categories against the likes of racing Porsches and D-Type Jaguars. Success always has its price.

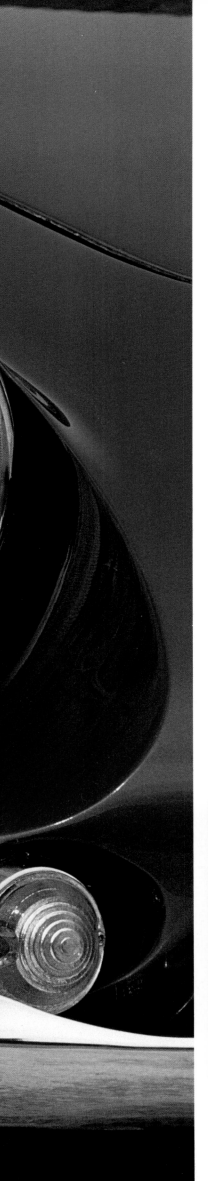

500 SUPERFAST

Ferrari didn't beat about the bush in naming his exclusive toy for the very rich and very choosy. It was simply Superfast. A giant step beyond the most powerful and exotic cars that Ferrari made for his 'ordinary' customers. A Pininfarina-styled extravaganza that made its own statement even when it was only parked. One of the most expensive cars in the world; the ultimate early '60s supercar. It has even been said that Ferrari saw the Superfast in the same way that Ettore Bugatti saw his Royale.

But it wasn't quite so simple as that. There wasn't just one Superfast, but a whole series of them, starting with an extraordinary flight of fancy by Pinin Farina at the 1956 Paris Show and culminating in a short 'production' run of this, the 500 Superfast, as announced at the Geneva Show in March 1964.

Between then and August 1966, when the lightly revised second series of 500s finally run out of mega-wealthy patrons, Ferrari built a total of thirty-seven 500 Superfasts to add to the five individual show cars that preceded it. He never made their like again, and nor really did anyone else.

To begin at the beginning, there was the 410 Super-america, itself launched in January 1956 as a replacement for the 375 America. It was the nearest thing around to a bespoke car, and through three main series hardly any two were exactly alike. They started on a long-wheelbase chassis, mainly bodied by Pinin Farina but with a coupé

each from Ghia and Boano and a cabrio from Boano too. Then came a series on a shorter chassis, all bar one Scaglietti car again being bodied by Pinin Farina. Finally there was a third series, with a number of engine and chassis changes but this time all bodied by Farina. The total run stretched to less than forty cars.

For the 1956 Paris Show, Pinin Farina (the name changed after 1958) transformed one of the early series Superamericas into a stunning confection which he called the Superfast. Maybe it was the most dramatic Ferrari ever built. It had a low roofline cantilevered forwards from swooping rear quarter pillars, but with no front pillars at all to break the curve of windscreen into side windows. It had huge tail fins, partly faired-in rear wheels, masses of chrome trim and a two-tone blue and white paint-job. Under the seemingly endless bonnet was the 380bhp twin-plug V12 from the racing 410 Sport. To call it sensational would be an understatement.

At Turin in 1957, Pinin Farina followed it up with the 4.9 Superfast, similarly powered and similar in looks except that it had lost the big tail fins and gained windscreen

The Superfast series started with a run of Pinin Farina show cars, and when it went into production in 1964, the 500 Superfast from Pininfarina was a striking car by any standards (below and overleaf), yet with a degree of restraint. It was less restrained under the skin; the long nose (left), with its single headlights and narrow oval grille, covered the biggest engine in any production Ferrari. . .

pillars. Next came Superfast II, at Turin in 1960, and again a Pininfarina project, not a Ferrari one. This time the underpinnings were from the 400 Superamerica, an all-new model launched in 1959 to replace the 410. The 400 'only' had a 4-litre Colombo-type engine and for some reason Ferrari sidestepped his usual scheme of numbering by the size of one cylinder and named this car for its total capacity.

Farina seems retrospectively to have lumped the first two Superfasts together as Superfast Is. Superfast II was less flamboyant and a step closer to a production possibility. Developed in the wind tunnel, its sleek, clean lines were the basis for the dozen or so 'Aerodinamica' coupés in the 400 Superamerica series which appeared soon after. It was also the starting point for the prototype GTOs . . .

Superfast III and Superfast IV both appeared in 1962, both in effect updatings of Superfast II, with different nose treatments. Superfast III was principally distinguished by retractable headlights, similar to the ones on Superfast II; Superfast IV chose a distinctive four-headlight layout that made the swooping nose look even longer and slimmer.

Then in 1964 at the Geneva Show the 500 Superfast emerged, not as a Pininfarina show model, although of course Pininfarina *had* styled it, but as a Ferrari production car. There was a good deal of 400 Superamerica in its lines but the pointed taper of the 400's tail was chopped short in Kamm style and the long nose was flanked by simple, uncovered lights.

Without doubt, the 500 Superfast, like the Superamerica, was a car aimed firmly at the far side of the Atlantic. Commercially, what was good for America was good for Ferrari, and what was good for America was generally bigger, faster and more conspicuously consumptive. America, after all, was home to the philosophy 'there's no substitute for cubic inches'. Eventually, public opinion would turn against the horsepower race but while it lasted Ferrari would give the people what they wanted. He might not sell too many Superfasts, but its aura would light up the cars that he *could* sell in reasonable numbers.

The engine in the 500 Superfast was unique to this model, and until the twin-turbocharged 2.8-litre V8 288GTO came along in 1984 it was the most powerful road car that Ferrari had ever built. The 500 stood for the capacity, virtually a full 5 litres; in fact at 4953cc, it remains the biggest capacity engine Ferrari has ever built for a road car, and almost the biggest engine he ever built of any kind. In that respect, it is beaten only by the 4994cc of the sports racing 512s, and the monstrous but short-lived 6222cc Can-Am V12 that Ferrari campaigned with little success in 1968 and 1969.

It was really neither a Colombo-type engine nor a Lampredi-type engine, but a blend of the two. It had the Lampredi long-block dimensions of the 410 Superamerica, but it had Colombo-type detachable cylinder heads, with the usual chain-drive single overhead camshaft to each bank. With three downdraught Weber carburettors, it produced 400bhp at 6500rpm, an extraordinary amount of power for a 1964 road car.

Its chassis was largely like the 330GT's, with coil-spring

. . . almost 5 litres of V12 (left) combining elements of both Colombo and Lampredi designs to produce a nice, round 400 bhp. That was quite enough to allow Ferrari to be generous with the trim (above) and the exterior decoration (far left), for his American customers.

and wishbone front suspension and a live rear axle on semi-elliptic springs, plus disc brakes all round. Early cars had four speeds plus an overdrive, later ones, reflecting changes in the 330s, had a true five-speed 'box. Customers had a wide choice of final drive ratios depending on whether they wanted blistering acceleration or long-legged cruising, and long-legged could mean anything up to around 160mph.

That was really its forte, high speeds on an open road where the broad-shouldered power could be opened up and where all the Ferrari virtues of road-feel and precision could shine through. Around town or on smaller lanes, it was a fish out of water, too big and too heavy in almost all its controls really to be fun, but then that wasn't what it was designed for; it made you work for your pleasures and, without wishing to appear sexist, it really was a man's car.

With such power on tap, at least Ferrari didn't have to skimp on the furnishings in the Superfast, and it combined its outstanding performance with the limousine-like luxuries of leather and wood and deep carpets; just the sort of surroundings that the type of customer who was paying perhaps double the price of a Rolls-Royce for a two-and-a-bit-seater grand tourer would have expected. And those customers, although there were only thirty-six of them across the two production series, were a pretty select bunch. Peter Sellers had a 500 Superfast, the Aga Khan had one, being as much an enthusiast for the Prancing Horse as for racing ones, and the Shah of Persia had two. In the rarefield world of the Superfasts, it seems, nothing succeeded like excess.

500 SUPERFAST SPECIFICATION

ENGINE
60° V12

CAPACITY
4962cc

BORE x STROKE
88.0 x 68.0mm

COMPRESSION RATIO
8.8:1

POWER
400bhp

VALVE GEAR
Single overhead camshafts

FUEL SYSTEM
Three Weber 40DCZ6 carburettors

TRANSMISSION
Five-speed manual

FRONT SUSPENSION
Independent, by double wishbones, coil springs, telescopic dampers

REAR SUSPENSION
Non-independent, by live axle, semi-elliptic leaf springs, parallel arms, telescopic dampers

BRAKES
All discs

WHEELS
Centre-lock wire

WEIGHT
c.3200lb (1451kg)

MAXIMUM SPEED
c.155mph (249kph)

NUMBER MADE, DATES
c.36, 1964–6

250LM

If Enzo Ferrari hadn't been a car constructor, he should probably have forgotten all his earlier ambitions as an opera singer or a sports journalist and made a wonderful career for himself as a politician.

He could hardly have failed. Throughout his life in motor sport, his skill as an interpreter (and often a manipulator) of the rules was legendary. Not always popular with his adversaries, but definitely legendary. It was a skill born of absolute belief in his own abilities, a refusal to suffer fools, gladly or otherwise; it was a fierce stubborness and autonomy, a genuine aura of power that even the rule makers sometimes couldn't resist, and – perversely perhaps – a wickedly mischievous delight in beating those rule makers at their own game.

He pulled in and out of races and championships with bombastic flourish to make his points. Sometimes his works car ran in private colours when the authorities had upset him. He argued with new formulae with the best of them before they came into force, but when the day came and other manufacturers were still arguing, Ferrari had the right new machinery on the grid anyway to run rings around them. Many opponents thought much of his political manipulation at best cynical and at worst actually rule-breaking, but to Ferrari it was all part of the game.

It failed him only rarely, but it failed him quite badly in one instance in the early 1960s, with the beautiful but ill-starred 250LM, the theoretically road-usable racer that should have been Ferrari's first mid-engined 'production' car but which fizzled out when Ferrari, for once, didn't beat the book.

The early 1960s were turbulent times at Maranello; finances were precarious and motor racing was heading into a period which would be dominated by science and by big money from over the Atlantic, in the shape of Ford's 'Total Performance' programme. Ford wanted nothing less than to win the Grand Prix World Championship, Indianapolis and Le Mans. By 1963, they had Lotus tackling the

The 250LM was one of Ferrari's more audacious attempts at getting round the rules, but one of the most beautiful cars of all (right). Had he really had any chance of homologating it, this could have been his first mid-engined road car.

The distinctive roofline of the 250LM (above and right) had first appeared on the last few 250GTOs, in 1964, and is all about improving aerodynamics, from its narrow frontal aspect to the deep tunnel which creates a low pressure area behind.

Indianapolis problem, but Ferrari was clearly in the way of the other two ambitions and Ford felt they had more money than time. Without going into too much detail, Ford, having recognised Ferrari's possible vulnerability to a stabilising source of finance at the time, tried to buy Ferrari out in 1963. By May, the deal had come very, very close to happening, with the prospect of Ford-Ferrari road cars and Ferrari-Ford racing cars; but then Ferrari told Ford that he would want to retain full control of all racing operations, Ford's US ones included, and the deal foundered mainly on that point.

Even that had a political overtone. Some years before, Carroll Shelby had been interviewed by Ferrari as a possible works driver, and suffered the apparent contempt with which Ferrari sometimes treated lesser mortals. Shelby, ambitious to build his own sports car, told Ferrari with admirable Texan clarity that one day he would be back 'to kick his ass'. By the time Ford tried to buy Ferrari, Shelby was wheeling out his Cobras under Ford patronage and winning. Ferrari could have become Shelby's boss . . .

Ford went away to develop their own GT40, Ferrari tried to re-open negotiations, but for a change it was he who was snubbed, and Shelby got on with his ass-kicking.

Between the two of them it turned into quite a game. In 1962 Ferrari had had the 250GTO homologated (even though he built only thirty-nine rather than the prescribed 100) by arguing that it was no more than a rebodied version of the existing 250GT SWB. In 1963 Shelby replied in kind by getting the Daytona coupé homologated as a re-bodied 289 Cobra – and only built seven of them! Ferrari countered in 1964 when Shelby looked close to winning the GT title with the Daytona by having the penultimate championship round, at Monza, cancelled, leaving Shelby with too few races to gain the points he still needed. In 1965, Ferrari withdrew from the championship part-way through the season, leaving Shelby's Daytonas with a victory they would probably have scored anyway, but rendered slightly hollow.

The main cooling vents for the mid-engine bay of the 250LM (left) were elegantly sculpted into the top of the rear wing lines by stylist Pininfarina, who also did a fine job in accommodating the huge length of the V12 without losing the balance.

Whatever the catalogue said, the 250LM was a racer, from its strictly functional cockpit (below left) to its massive fuel fillers (bottom left) and the way the whole tail lifted (below and bottom) for rapid access to all the most important bits.

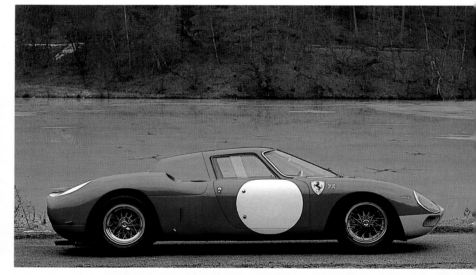

Midships mounting for the big V12 challenged Ferrari's packaging skills (left) even more than usual. Only the first engine was actually a 3-litre; all the rest were 3.3s, but Ferrari never advertised the fact by changing the type number.

The reason that Ferrari withdrew in 1965 was that for once the FIA had drawn a line and refused to homologate the 250LM. Probably a little optimistically, even in the light of the previous two years' shenanigans, Ferrari had tried in 1964 to have the 250LM (LM for Le Mans, of course) accepted as just another evolution of the 250GTO. The FIA had fallen for the GTO and the Daytona, but they certainly weren't going to fall for a mid-engined 'variant' of a front-engined car. And to rub it in even further, only the first prototype had actually been a 250LM; all subsequent cars should really have been labelled 275LM, because Ferrari had surreptitiously increased the capacity of the Colombo V12 again to 3.3 litres, but without aggravating matters further by changing the type number!

The 250LM itself was rather more than incidental. Relegated to running as a prototype, against the GT40s, it was outclassed, but had Ferrari managed to wangle it into the GT class as intended, it could have been a different story, even against Shelby's Daytonas.

Rather than evolving from the 250GTs, it had really grown out of the 1963 250P, a car designed to run under that year's Le Mans-sponsored sub-category for 'sports prototypes'. That was in effect a 3-litre Testa Rossa V12 shoehorned into a Dino 246SP mid-engined chassis – the first 'full-sized' mid-engined sports racer that Ferrari had built and clearly the shape of the future. Four 250Ps were built and they did the trick by winning Le Mans (twice if you include the 275P win in 1964) and many other races. The 250LM has been described as 'a 250P with a roof'.

It undoubtedly looked that way and there are some who would say its voluptuously sleek Pininfarina-styled shape is one of the most beautiful of all. Beneath it was a complex spaceframe chassis rather than the relatively simple ladder of the GTs, and independent suspension all round, by coil springs and wishbones, where the GTs still had live rear axles. All but the first had a 3.3-litre Colombo V12, delivering around 320bhp through a five-speed transaxle. Although it was clearly a racing car, with a desperately cramped and spartan cockpit and no proper luggage space, Ferrari went through the motions of listing it as a GT model, suitable for the road. Of the thirty two built, two were actually finished with rather better trim and equipment and a few hardier racing owners did venture onto the highway occasionally.

Rules and regulations and political points-scoring notwithstanding, Ferrari had the last laugh with the LM. At Le Mans in 1965, Jochen Rindt and Masten Gregory were entered in a 250LM run by Luigi Chinetti's North American Racing Team, NART. They were entered as a prototype, of course, and consequently facing the GT40s, which very few sensible people would have bet against. Resigned to being also rans, they simply kept driving the LM as hard as they could while the faster cars drew steadily away, content to pick up whatever placing they could. But then the faster cars began to fall by the wayside until the Rindt/Gregory LM was left to cruise home to a memorable victory, followed by two more Ferraris in second and third places. Every GT40 retired, and just one of Shelby's five Daytonas survived, to finish eighth overall, beaten into second place in the GT class by another Ferrari. Although all his works cars had retired too, Enzo Ferrari must have been able to raise a smile.

250LM (275LM)
SPECIFICATION

ENGINE
60° V12

CAPACITY
2953cc (3286cc)

BORE x STROKE
73.0 x 58.8mm (77.0 x 58.8mm)

COMPRESSION RATIO
9.7:1

POWER
300bhp (320bhp)

VALVE GEAR
Single overhead camshafts

FUEL SYSTEM
Six Weber 38DCN carburettors

TRANSMISSION
Five-speed manual

FRONT SUSPENSION
Independent, by double wishbones, coil springs, telescopic dampers

REAR SUSPENSION
Independent, by double wishbones, coil springs, telescopic dampers

BRAKES
All discs

WHEELS
Centre-lock wire

WEIGHT
c.1900lb (861kg)

MAXIMUM SPEED
c.160mph (257kph)

NUMBER MADE, DATES
35, 1963-6

275GTB

The all-new car that Ferrari launched at the Paris Show late in 1964 was one of the most radical pure road cars that he had offered in quite some time. It was nothing less than the start of a new generation, finally superseding the faithful 250 family that had been Ferrari's staple for over a decade. It was a car to continue the 250 tradition, certainly, but it was also a car to bring the tradition up to date. In theory it would still offer the dual-purpose nature of earlier cars, but with a bit more comfort again and a few less ragged edges. And as far as possible it would rationalise the range into one elegant body shape, designed by Pininfarina, of course.

Or to be completely accurate, two elegant body shapes, because alongside the 275GTB coupé Ferrari would simultaneously launch the 275GTS spyder, with identical chassis, apparently identical yet slightly less powerful engine and a look of its own.

The two were visually quite different; the GTB look was all-new, softly rounded and as air-cheatingly smooth as could be; the GTS, only ever intended as a touring car and so with less call for ultimate aerodynamics, was more of a carry-over, squarer cut and with more ornament, a cross between a 250 spyder and a 330GT 2+2 perhaps. Scaglietti built the bodies for the berlinettas, Pininfarina themselves built those for the spyders.

Ferrari, of course, built the chassis and engines, in Maranello, and there was plenty that was new in their side of the 275s too. The first 275GTB was the last of the berlinetta line to use a single-overhead-camshaft version of the long-serving Colombo 'short-block' V12, but it was another stage bigger; and far from being in its final throes, with its new additional capacity it was still an extremely fine engine.

The new size, 3285cc, or near enough 275cc per cylinder for the sake of a convenient model made, was arrived at by increasing the bore yet again – this time to what seemed certain to be its final stretch. The stroke was left the same as in the 250s, so the 275 engine was even more oversquare than its predecessor and even more flexible.

In another respect, the 275GTB, and the 275GTS spyder, represented not just an update but a seminal advance for Ferrari.

That was in its chassis technology.

As late as 1964, Ferrari was still relying on non-independent rear suspension on his road cars, generally with nothing more sophisticated than a live rear axle hung on semi-elliptic 'cart' springs and further located by parallel trailing arms. With the 275GTB (and the GTS) he finally adopted for the road the sort of fully independent suspension that his racing models had been using for years, and which new arch-rival Lamborghini had designed onto his very first model – the 350GT that he showed off in Turin in 1963. Now, both ends of the new Ferrari used the highly effective layout of unequal length upper and lower wishbones, with coil springs, and telescopic dampers, just like the racers and offering much better rear-end control.

As well as the new suspension, the move away from a live rear axle allowed Ferrari to rethink the rest of the drivetrain layout, and now instead of being in unit with the engine the five-speed gearbox reappeared at the rear of the car, in unit with the final drive, as a transaxle. All that was now left at the engine end was the clutch and its bellhousing.

In one swoop that made for a more compact transmission

By the time the 275GTB was launched, science was aiding simple power in motor sport, and in these magnificently sleek lines (far left) it isn't hard to see the new emphasis on aerodynamics. Quarter windows (left) are signs of an early example.

tunnel and hence better passenger space, as well as a better balanced car. The one thing it didn't do, unfortunately, was to retain the beautiful precision of the earlier gear-changes, as the direct communication with the 'box was replaced by a longer and rather notchy linkage.

Nor did Ferrari get the new design quite right first time and on the berlinetta – though never on the spyder – he first changed the propshaft joints then eventually added a torque tube (a rigid connection between engine and transaxle, with the propellor shaft running through it) to cure problems of alignment.

All in all, it added up to a car that was both beautiful to look at and superb to drive, combining the comforts of the Lusso with the sporting image of, say, the Short-Wheelbase Berlinetta. It was capable of not far short of 150mph (241kph), but that revealed the other early shortcoming, a worrying tendency for the very short nose to lift a speed. As well as other minor body changes in 1965, the 275GTB was given a longer nose to tackle that, and naturally, many owners wanted to race with the car . . .

Although he didn't do it in quite the same way, with a totally separate line of cars like the old Tour de France berlinettas or the 250GTO, Ferrari did offer competition versions of the 275GTB alongside the mainstream model. The standard car had a steel shell with aluminium doors, boot and bonnet and around 280bhp on tap from its three-carb engine. Alternatively, Ferrari offered an optional six-carburettor engine which wasn't quite so flexible as the normal unit but which offered maybe another 20bhp. Beyond that, a very small number, just over a dozen or so, of more seriously competition-minded 275GTBs was made in 1964 and 1965. These were more or less built to individual specifications but typically with rather lighter bodywork (most of them, oddly, to the original short-nose pattern) and the six-carburettor engines, a handful of them using dry-sump versions.

Over and above those cars, Ferrari offered another variant

The rear quarter vents (above) kept the well-trimmed cockpit cool, and the alloy wheels (right) were a roadgoing first.

of the 275GTB in 1966, intended purely for GT racing. That was known as the 275GTB/C, with the C obviously standing for *competizione*; and Ferrari, possibly still smarting from the FIA's rejection of the 250LM, was careful not to bend the rules too far. So aside from a slight flare to the wheelarches (and the fact that it didn't have the torque tube), the 275GTB/C looked much like any other long-nosed 275GTB; but it was lighter, thanks to extra-thin all-aluminium bodywork and perspex side and rear windows; and it was more powerful, with special cams, bigger valves and dry sumps – although the increase in power was slightly limited by the fact that only the three-carb set-up was homologated.

Having built over 450 275GTBs, eleven 275GTB/Cs, and some 200 GTSs up to 1966, Ferrari dropped the competition model and the spyder (replacing the latter with the 330GTS) but launched an even more impressive version of the berlinetta, predictably enough at his favourite Paris Show, in 1966, exactly two years after the first 275GTB had appeared.

On top of the all-independent, all disc-brake chassis with its rear transaxle and torque tube, this one had another major first. It had the first Ferrari road car engine with double overhead camshafts to each cylinder bank. It could

rev a bit harder, and with the six-carburettor set-up and dry sump lubrication as standard, it squeezed the power right up to 300bhp at no less than 8000rpm.

That gave the 275GTB/4, as the car was now known, a top speed of well over 150mph (241kph), but also wonderful flexibility and refinement. Best of all, the performance was entirely usable, and many people who have driven the 275GTBs, two-cam or four-cam, will tell you that with their mixture of ample, well-spread power, compact dimensions, light weight and excellent new suspension, they were both fast and flatteringly easy to drive. Ferrari built another 350 or so four-cam cars through 1966 and 1967 (and ten 275GTB/4 spyders – actually GTB-based this time – were built to special order for Luigi Chinetti, Ferrari's US east coast distributor and boss of the North American Racing Team), but then the 275GTB/4 was replaced by the 365GTB/4, the Daytona. What a choice to have to make.

The first generation of 275GTBs had a two-cam engine (right) rather than the four cams of the later 275GTB/4, and the six-carburettor set-up was optional rather than standard, but in this form the two-cam engine gave away very little in power. The nose of the 275GTB (left) was lengthened to cure early cars' tendency to lift, but the aerodynamics of the Kamm tail (top), gave no problems.

275GTB SPECIFICATION

ENGINE
60° V12

CAPACITY
3286cc

BORE x STROKE
77.0 × 58.8mm

COMPRESSION RATIO
9.2:1

POWER
250bhp

VALVE GEAR
Single overhead camshafts

FUEL SYSTEM
Three Weber 40DCZ6 carburettors

TRANSMISSION
Five-speed manual

FRONT SUSPENSION
Independent, by double wishbones, coil springs, telescopic dampers

REAR SUSPENSION
Independent, by double wishbones, coil springs, telescopic dampers

BRAKES
All discs

WHEELS
Centre-lock wire

WEIGHT
c.2900lb (1315kg)

MAXIMUM SPEED
c.150mph (241kph)

NUMBER MADE, DATES
c.455, 1964–6

330GTS

The mid-1960s were healthy days indeed for the sale of drophead Ferraris, but they were also the days just before America started to embrace the *Unsafe at Any Speed* thinking of the safety lobby, and to frown on some of the things that true sports car enthusiasts like best; things like uncompromised power and unrestricted fresh air.

We moaned at the time, and some people have been moaning ever since, but in one respect the environmentalists were right; if we hadn't done something to control the former, we couldn't hope to enjoy the latter because in the early 1960s power all too often meant pollution.

The market changed, too, thanks to simple economics as well as to noble protectionism, as one 'oil crisis' succeeded another, and gas-guzzling cars became outcasts.

Ferrari responded initially with bigger but less stressed engines, with four cams and acceptably cleaner emissions, but then the rules got tougher and Ferrari, for a while, got his big cars out of America. But Ferrari's problem applied to everyone, and to the motor industry's lasting credit it rose to the challenge and cleaned up its act; then, having learned how to make clean engines, it started to learn how to make clean, powerful engines again – Ferrari included.

Another aspect of the new puritanism was almost as fundamental; America could no longer trust open-topped cars, reasoning that when the inevitable happened and you landed your car on its roof, it would be better if there really was a roof to land on. So without ever actually banning soft-tops, the Land of the Free left manufacturers to listen to their product liability lawyers and draw their own conclusions, and the conclusions generally were that if soft-tops weren't dangerous physically, they were horribly dangerous politically, and they had to go.

Sadly for Europe, sales of soft-tops were so massively dependent on sales to the sunny West Coast that if a manufacturer couldn't sell to America he couldn't afford to sell at all. Thus, between the short run of Daytona Spyders which ended in 1973 and the Mondial Cabriolet which appeared in 1984, Ferrari didn't build a true convertible. And setting the Daytona Spyder aside as something of an

The 330GTS offered all the comforts of the GTC coupé, plus the option of fresh air (right), in a handsomely discreet package (overleaf) designed for real touring.

anachronism, the last important soft-tops before the Mondial were the ones from the 1960s.

That highly successful family started with the 275GTS in 1964 and ran profitably through the rest of the 1960s until the 365GTS went out of production in 1969. Across three series Ferrari sold some 320 examples, most of them, naturally, to the USA. The beauty of them was that they were straightforward and unfussy cars, compact, and with functional rather than over-lavish interiors, discreet in looks yet still individual enough to be very desirable.

The 275GTS launched the series at the Paris Show (inevitably) in October 1964. Alongside the new 275GTB, it represented Ferrari middle-ground, sharing the same 94½-inch wheelbase and 3.3-litre Colombo V12, but with conservative styling all its own more like a topless cousin of the 330GT 2+2 than a topless sister to the 275GTB, but with the single headlight layout that didn't appear on the 2+2 until 1965 rather than the unloved twin headlights of the 1963 original.

It was slightly more conservative than the 275GTB in power output too, with 260bhp compared to 275, and in the chassis, which gained the jointed propshaft but never the torque tube eventually used on the GTB to cure drivetrain alignment problems. It was meant as a comfortable, fast, open tourer, not as a racer.

Ferrari sold exactly 200 275GTSs up to May 1966, so when they officially replaced the 275GTS with the 330GTS, at Paris in the autumn of 1966, Ferrari already knew they were onto a winner. The 330GTS was more than just the usual bigger-engine progression, though. The angular nose of the 275 had given way to a rounder, less toothy look apparently inspired by the prestigious 500 Superfast, and just as on the sister 330GTC. Under the skin, this GTS spyder actually was a convertible version of the coupé, as introduced at the Geneva Show in March 1966. As such, it was quite different from the 275GTS. The chassis did now adopt the rigid torque tube between front engine and rear five-speed transaxle, with the four-point rubber-block mountings that contributed to markedly lower cockpit noise levels.

That meant that the 4-litre 'long-block' Colombo V12 from the 330GT 2+2 had to have its mounts slightly modified but otherwise it was much the same unit. This time it had gained capacity by a lengthening of its stroke (within deeper blocks) via a new crankshaft, rather than by increasing the bore again. The latter was feasible in that the bore spacings had been increased for better cooling and hence better reliability for racing, but it was not yet desirable. The new engine (still generically referred to as a Colombo even though so little now remained) was much less oversquare than the 275s, but just as effective. With three downdraught Weber carburettors it gave a nice round 300bhp at a comparitively understressed 7000rpm – soothingly less in an open car than the frenetic 8000rpm required for the same power in the four-cam 3.3-litre 375GTB/4.

With 40bhp more to hand than the four-cam 275GTS, the new car was not much quicker in terms of maximum speed, which stayed around 145mph (233kph), but was a

Disc brakes behind the Borrani wheels (opposite) were now normal spec for Ferraris and the general outline of the 275GTS had really only changed in the longer nose (left) but the full convertible layout (above) worried the new safety lobby in America.

good deal more lively and flexible in getting there.

For a full convertible, and a heavy one too, it was quite quick enough but the now very refined chassis, with coil spring and double wishbone suspension all round and all disc brakes, could handle it with ease. It genuinely was a car in which you could chase the sun.

Up to late 1968, Ferrari added 100 examples of the 330GTS to the 200 275GTSs they had previously sold. The numbers were relatively small alongside, say, around 600 330GTCs, but they were the most Ferrari had ever made of any soft-top series up to that time.

The bubble effectively burst with the 330GTS even though as the aforementioned American problems began to make themselves felt, Ferrari went through the motions late in 1968 when he duly produced a 365GTS spyder alongside the 365GTC coupé, just as he had with the 330s. He had already dropped the apparently conflicting 365 California spyder after building barely more than a dozen copies, but in truth that just wasn't a particularly good car, with the old layout of engine and gearbox in unit and in a chassis that was too long and still burdened with the old non-independent rear suspension.

The 365GTS was a very much better proposition than the California but it ran into other problems. It was dropped in the middle of 1969, after only about twenty cars had been built, supposedly in favour of the 365GTB/4 Daytona. It's pretty hard to see any way that the Daytona offered anything comparable to the 365GTS, but it's less difficult to see that the Daytona did have a cleaner, four-cam engine, a hard roof and a long-term future in America.

**330GTS
SPECIFICATION**

ENGINE
60° V12

CAPACITY
3967cc

BORE x STROKE
77.0 x 71.0mm

COMPRESSION RATIO
8.8:1

POWER
300bhp

VALVE GEAR
Single overhead camshafts

FUEL SYSTEM
Three Weber 40DCZ6 carburettors

TRANSMISSION
Five-speed manual

FRONT SUSPENSION
Independent, by double wishbones, coil springs, telescopic dampers

REAR SUSPENSION
Independent, by double wishbones, coil springs, telescopic dampers

BRAKES
All discs

WHEELS
Centre-lock wire

WEIGHT
c.3400lb (1542kg)

MAXIMUM SPEED
c.145mph (233kph)

NUMBER MADE, DATES
c.100, 1966–8

365GTB/4
DAYTONA

By 1968, Ferrari had a new and serious rival in the supercar stakes, and one whose willingness to embrace new ideas was in rather stark contrast to Ferrari's own sometimes frustrating conservatism. The new rival had even supposedly gone into the sports car business in the first place in the early 1960s because of the treatment he had received from Enzo Ferrari at first hand.

The pretender was a tractor-maker from the Ferrara district of northern Italy, born barely 20 miles from where Ferrari himself had been born, and now with a modern and successful supercar factory virtually on Maranello's door-step, just east of Modena at Sant'Agata Bolognese. He had personally owned Ferraris that had proved troublesome and unrefined for everyday use, had told Ferrari so, and been dismissed as a mere agricultural engineer and unfit to judge a true thoroughbred.

Allegedly on the strength of that treatment he went off to beat Ferrari at his own game, and by the late 1960s the world at large obviously thought he was making some progress. Yet if Enzo Ferrari was troubled by the upstart Ferrucio Lamborghini, he wasn't about to show it; Lamborghini, after all, wouldn't take up the gauntlet on the racing circuit, and even if Lamborghini *had* set the world alight with the sensationally advanced, mid-engined Miura in 1966, Ferrari wasn't about to follow suit.

Of course, Ferrari *could* have built a mid-engined road car; he had, after all, been building mid-engined single-seaters since 1960, and mid-engined sports racing cars since 1961. Pininfarina had shown the first mid-engined Dino Berlinetta styling exercise at the Paris Show in October 1985, and the 206GT Dino road car would actually be in production by early 1968; but when the magnificent 365GTB/4 was introduced, in Paris later in 1968, its glorious V12 was unashamedly in the front, and the car was as overtly conservative as the Miura was controversial.

Yet anyone who despaired of Ferrari forsaking the chance to slip into the modern idiom purely because he didn't want

The Daytona (right and overleaf) might have lagged behind the contemporaneous Lamborghini Miura in its front-engined technology, but not in performance, and Pininfarina made it one of the most aggressive looking of all Ferrari road cars.

to be seen as following the upstart Lamborghini, would have been seriously wide of the mark. The new Daytona, as it quickly came to be known (and the most expensive production model that Ferrari had so far offered), was a hugely practical and comfortable grand tourer, delightful to drive over long distances and demanding no exceptional skills. It was reliable, utterly beautiful, and Miura or no Miura it was the fastest production car in the world.

By 1968, the new car *was* needed. By then, its predecessor, the lovely 275GTB/4, as launched in 1964, had been caught not only by Lamborghini but also to a lesser extent by far less thoroughbred offerings from the likes of Bizzarrini, Iso and Maserati. The 275 itself had been a fine car, the first production Ferrari with all-independent suspension, the first with a five-speed rear transaxle layout, a Ferrari with rather more concessions to creature comfort than any before; but now there was no more scope for development in its 3.3-litre Colombo-type V12, and hence no further scope to keep up in the performance race.

So the 365GTB/4 (365 for the individual cylinder capacity, GTB for *Gran Turismo Berlinetta*, 4 for the number of camshafts) was penned around a new version of Aurelio Lampredi's 60°, short-stroke, 'long-block' V12 – a basic design which dated back to the early 1950s but which had life in it yet. With those four chain-driven overhead camshafts, a total capacity of 4390cc, and fed by six twin-choke downdraught Weber carburettors, the new V12 gave

handsomely more power than the 275GTB/4's 300bhp best – up in the Daytona to 352bhp at 7500rpm, with a wonderfully flexible nature (peaking with 318lb ft of torque at 5500rpm), and a nice, clean exhaust emission to keep the US market happy.

That compared, incidentally, with a claimed 350bhp for the contemporaneous Miura, so until the rather special 370bhp Miura S of 1970 came along, Ferrari was pointedly back in front in the horsepower race.

The Daytona was built on the same wheelbase as the 275GTB/4, styled by Pininfarina, of course, bodied for production by Scaglietti, and very little larger overall than its predecessor. On early Daytonas, four fixed headlamps were set behind a full-width plexiglass nose section, but the US market didn't approve of that, so it soon gave way to a more universally acceptable, pop-up headlamp system. With such add-ons, a largely steel body (with aluminium only for the doors, boot and bonnet lids) and the bigger engine, the Daytona wasn't quite as lightweight as the 275, but the potent Lampredi engine kept the power-to-weight ratio up around the 220bhp per ton mark and the enormous torque meant that overall flexibility was in a totally different league.

With an independently tested maximum of 174mph (279kph) and the ability to reach 60mph (97kph) in 5.4 seconds and 100mph (161kph) in just 12.6 seconds, the Daytona put Ferrari well ahead of all-comers once again.

The unmistakable look of the Daytona is dominated by the long bonnet, the short, cropped tail and the high waistline. By the time the Daytona came along, tyres were growing much wider too, and alloy wheels had almost completely replaced wires.

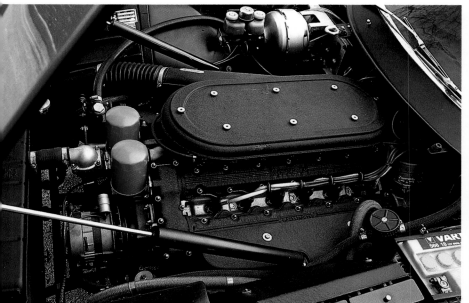

Rolling sculpture: inside and out, the Daytona was a tour de force by Pininfarina and Ferrari alike, for the superb driving environment, the lovely detail design and, of course, the hugely powerful four-cam V12 – the last of a glorious line.

365GTB/4 DAYTONA SPECIFICATION

ENGINE
60° V12

CAPACITY
4390cc

BORE x STROKE
81.0 × 71.0mm

COMPRESSION RATIO
9.3:1

POWER
352bhp

VALVE GEAR
Double overhead camshafts

FUEL SYSTEM
Six Weber 40DCN carburettors

TRANSMISSION
Five-speed manual

FRONT SUSPENSION
Independent, by double wishbones, coil springs, telescopic dampers

REAR SUSPENSION
Independent, by double wishbones, coil springs, telescopic dampers

BRAKES
All discs

WHEELS
Centre-lock alloy

WEIGHT
c.3900lb (1769kg)

MAXIMUM SPEED
c.174mph (279kph)

NUMBER MADE, DATES
c.1285 coupés, 127 spyders, 1968–74

And if the Daytona was front-engined, it was at least front-engined with science. The big aluminium block was set as far back in the tubular chassis as it would go, and the five-speed transaxle followed the lead set by the 275 by sitting at the rear, all of which contributed to a near perfect front-to-rear weight distribution of around 52/48. The all-independent suspension was by the familiar double-wishbone and coil springs all round, with anti-roll bars at front and rear, and the brakes were all discs.

Thus equipped, the Daytona was one of the finest handling of all 'conventional' supercars – very heavy at the helm at low speeds but delightfully lighter at speed, probably as tenacious in its grip as the Miura, and certainly more forgiving in both its tail-end manners around the limits adhesion and its front-end manners around the limits of aerodynamic lift. In virtually any realistic driving situation on real roads it was almost unquestionably the fastest car of its day overall, yet with the comfort and luggage-carrying practicality of a real grand tourer.

And just to rub in the point to Lamborghini, the Daytona did something the Miura never did – it went racing, always privately entered, hampered admittedly in

the increasingly sophisticated sports car ranks by its weight and frankly marginal brakes, but good enough in 'light-weight' 450bhp trim to finish in fifth to ninth places overall at Le Mans as late as 1972, and to take second overall at Daytona in 1979!

The Daytona underwent few changes through its production life; few were needed. The one major event was the introduction of the Spyder version, the 365GTS/4, at the Frankfurt Show in 1969. Nowadays, the Spyders command vastly inflated prices, even to the extent that many an innocent coupé has been decapitated for no better reason than to increase its value, but less than 130 customers took the soft-top option originally, from a total of around 1400 Daytona sales.

Production ended in 1974, and with it the era of the front-engined Ferrari supercar also came to a close. Ferrari has built front-engined V12s since, in the four-seater 400 and 412 series, but the Daytona was the last of a great line; when its successor, the first Berlinetta Boxer, appeared in 1974, the engine was in the middle, but very few would dispute that Ferrari's final front-engined fling had been anything but a triumph.

117

365GTC

In Ferrari terms, the 365GTC was something of a wallflower, in production for barely a year, with only 150 examples made, and seen by many enthusiasts as boringly conservative. But those who know the car better cite it as one of the finest all-rounders that Maranello ever built.

Maybe its main problem was that it arrived, late in 1968, at just the same time as the considerably higher-profile 365GTB/4 Daytona, a car fit to overshadow almost anything. Or maybe the drawback was just the old one of familiarity breeding contempt, because when the 365GTC and the mechanically identical 365GTS spyder (of which only around twenty were built) were introduced, they weren't really presented as anything more than bigger-engined versions of the long-running 330 equivalents.

The 330s had been around since early 1966, and by Ferrari standards even they hadn't really been presented as anything spectacularly new, more as a clever re-blending of existing ingredients; to whit, the 275GTB chassis and the 4-litre V12 engine as previously seen, since the beginning of 1964, in the 330GT 2+2.

Even the new 4.4-litre engine which gave the 365s their traditional designation wasn't exactly hot news, because that had already been available in the 330GT 2+2's successor, the 365GT 2+2 since its Paris Show debut in 1967. The Colombo 'long-block' engine appeared in the two-seater 365s with nothing much more than minor modifications to the carburation. The chassis, too, was almost a direct carry-over from the 330s', save for some minor updating and a different make of disc brake. So, good as it was, that wasn't going to get a new avalanche of buyers excited either. And then there was the carry-over styling.

Just about the only touch of flamboyance or aggression in the 330GTC had been the big three-louvred air-vents behind the front wheelarches, designed to let hot air out from under the bonnet space. On the 365GTC, in spite of its bigger engine, even those had disappeared, to be replaced by less ostentatious vents in the bonnet just ahead of the windscreen scuttle. Beyond that, the Pininfarina shape was unchanged from the 330s', and again in inevitable comparison with the ultra-glamorous Daytona it was seen as rather dull. Worse still, the recent introduction of the diminutive but at least excitingly different mid-engined Dino didn't do the 365GTC's image much good, and there was a feeling right from the start that here was a car simply marking time until the next generation.

The styling of the 365GTC was almost unchanged from that of the 330GTC, from its long and slender 400 Superamerica-like nose (left) to its high-waisted profile (overleaf), but these cars of the late 1960s looked noticeably chunkier now than earlier Ferraris, largely thanks to the coming of the new generation of wider, lower-profile tyres on alloy rather than the long-favoured wire wheels.

That, frankly, did it scant justice.

It wasn't a totally integrated piece of styling, but there is something rather beautiful about its simplicity. In its delicacy of line, if not in its actual shape, the low roofline with its slender pillars and large wraparound glass areas had more than a hint of the 250GT Berlinetta Lusso about it; the long and slender nose, tapering towards a neat oval grille and with exposed headlamps set well back on either side, was clearly lifted from the 400 Superamerica; and the short, droopy tail (much squarer and chunkier than the curvaceous nose) was almost straight from the 275GTS. Executed by some styling houses, such a jigsaw puzzle of styles might have been a disaster, but Pininfarina's surefire touch made it work.

It *wasn't* the most spectacular looking Ferrari ever made but it wasn't intended to be. Genuine grand touring civility was the 365GTC's long suit. It was unashamedly a car built as much for comfort as for speed. It was spacious, light and airy inside, a pure two-seater but with ample luggage capacity for two and all the creature comforts to make it practicable for everyday long distance transport.

More than most contemporaneous Ferraris, it could almost be called luxurious. It had the usual leather trim, naturally, and it had a wooden dashboard which distinguished it from the more competition-oriented cars. It had nicely fitted carpets and ample soundproofing behind them, which made it quite feasible to listen to the fitted radio even at reasonable cruising speeds, where in many Ferraris you couldn't even hear yourself think. The torque-tube chassis layout carried over from the 330 (and ultimately from the 275GTB) helped with the refinement, too, as well as giving the 365s superb ride and handling. With the engine linked to the rear transaxle by the rigid torque tube, the whole drivetrain needed only four solid rubber mounting points between it and the chassis and that dramatically cut down transmission of mechanical noise and vibrations. More than one contemporary road tester considered the 330 and 365's new-found quietness to be the most significant advance over earlier Ferraris.

The 365GTC even listed air-conditioning and electric windows as options, yet for all that it didn't sacrifice true Ferrari performance and poise. The engine was the up-scaled version of the faithful Colombo design that had made the 330 possible, a shade longer in the block to allow for slightly wider bore spacing and hence bigger bores, and a touch deeper to accommodate longer stroke, but still conveniently more compact than the big-block Lampredi alternative. The yet-bigger 365 engine was more powerful again, of course, with 320bhp compared to the 330GTC's 300, at 6600 rather than 7000rpm, while it had a useful increase in torque, to 267lb ft, all of which made the 365 a delightfully flexible and rapid proposition.

Alongside the 600 or so examples of the 330GTC built in the three years before the 365 came onto the scene, the 150 cars in the 365GTC run looks rather meagre; and the mere twenty copies of the 365GTS spyder looks even less impressive alongside the approximately 100-strong output of its 330GTS predecessor.

The 365GTS was officially phased out to switch production capacity to the Daytona, but it is probably also significant that, with the exception of the small run of Daytona Spyders started in 1969, the 365 spyder was the last proper soft-top Ferrari (as distinct from the targa-style Dino and 308/328 spyders) until the Mondial Cabriolet came along in October 1983; and the 365GTC was the last of the full-size luxury GTs.

The real truth is that the 365s were simply cars that had arrived slightly late for the party. Good as they were (and they *were* good), their type of front-engined two-seater coupé and spyder just weren't the kind of car that Ferrari could justify commercially anymore. Their all-important place in the American market was fast being closed down by burgeoning safety and anti-pollution regulations that the graciously ageing model couldn't economically be made to meet; if Ferrari couldn't sell them in large numbers in America that rather did for the tiny European production.

So the Daytona, much more environmentally adaptable with its four-cam, cylinder heads and rather more modern design, could be left to carry the flag at the top of the range, in America too, and Ferrari could start to make some money from volume sales of the Dino, even if he couldn't bring himself to put his name on it.

**365GTC
SPECIFICATION**

ENGINE
60° V12

CAPACITY
4390cc

BORE x STROKE
81.0 x 71.0mm

COMPRESSION RATIO
8.8:1

POWER
320bhp

VALVE GEAR
Single overhead camshafts

FUEL SYSTEM
Three Weber 40DCN carburettors

TRANSMISSION
Five-speed manual

FRONT SUSPENSION
Independent, by double wishbones, coil springs, telescopic dampers

REAR SUSPENSION
Independent, by double wishbones, coil springs, telescopic dampers

BRAKES
All discs

WHEELS
Centre-lock alloy

WEIGHT
c.3600lb (1632kg)

MAXIMUM SPEED
c.150mph (241kph)

NUMBER MADE, DATES
c.150, 1968–70

The 365GTC was a genuinely luxurious two-seater tourer, spacious and comfortable (far left), with the practical bonus of excellent all-round visibility thanks to its thin roof pillars and wraparound glass (below). Externally, only the bonnet vents (left) were new.

246GT
DINO

One of the most significant cars that Ferrari ever made started life with neither the Ferrari name nor the Prancing Horse logo anywhere to be seen around its radically novel body. It didn't have twelve cylinders either, only six, and it was the first purely roadgoing car from Maranello to have its engine behind the driver rather than in front. It had been led into production by a mass-produced and conventionally front-engined sibling from Fiat, a good two years before Fiat took commercial control of Ferrari; and it started a direct line of smaller cars from Ferrari that lasted in practice right into the mid-1970s, and in spirit perhaps even beyond that.

It was the Dino, presaged by a Pininfarina styling exercise labelled the Dino Berlinetta, which was shown at the Paris Show in October 1965, another called the Dino Berlinetta GT at the Turin Show in November 1966, and eventually launched in virtually production form at the next Turin Show exactly a year later. By the middle of 1968 it was into production as the Dino 206GT, and through three series of 246GT, in coupé and spyder variants, it ran until 1974 when it was replaced by the eight-cylinder 308GT4 – a Ferrari in name once again, but perhaps a Dino by nature.

For Enzo Ferrari, the Dino line was at once an opportunity to introduce an easier to build, bigger selling and more profitable product, without offending those inevitable purists who would say anything with less than twelve cylinders would debase the Ferrari name; to homologate a 'mass-produced' engine for a new Formula 2; and to pay tribute to his dead son.

Alfredo was Ferrari's only legitimate son, the son who he had expected to take over his mantle; Alfredino was the affectionate name for little Alfredo, Dino was the nickname that stuck. He was born in January 1932, when his father was still a racing driver, and it was his birth which prompted Enzo finally to abandon racing for the safer career

Faced with the challenge of a smaller, mid-engined car, Pininfarina showed his genius – with a shape whose daring 'flying buttress' rear window line (right) and shark nose (overleaf) look as stunning in this 246GT as they did over 20 years ago.

NUMBER MADE, DATES
c.4000 (inc. 246GTS spyder),
1969–74

just 150 cars built before it was superseded by the 246GT late in 1969.

The new number indicated rather more than just a size increase to 2.4 litres. To help Fiat over production problems, it used a cast-iron block which made it a bit heavier, but it

Carlo Rally as late as 1979. During that time, the Dino gained a universal reputation for outstanding handling, the need for additional production capacity added a new 100,000sq ft wing to Maranello, and Fiat assumed the role of proprietor. The Dino was hardly a Ferrari also-ran . . .

c.145mph (233kph)

NUMBER MADE, DATES
c.4000 (inc. 246GTS spyder),
1969–74

as team manager that led to him building first his own racing cars and ultimately the whole Ferrari empire.

By the time Ferrari started building Ferraris, Dino was in his 'teens and being groomed to work with and eventually inherit from his father. He studied engineering at the Corni Institute in Modena and commerce at the University of

The biggest change between first prototypes and the production Dino was in the nose (left and below). The show car's four headlights and full-width plexiglass cover look awfully dated now, the definitive version

365GT4/BB
'BERLINETTA BOXER'

With the official launch of the 365GT4/BB at the Paris Salon in 1973, Enzo Ferrari made a major break with his previously staunch traditionalism, and a timely move towards more contemporary thinking. Not only was the 365GT4/BB a wholly new car, new virtually from the ground up, but it was also the start of a completely new philosophy for Ferrari's road cars.

This was a quantum leap for Maranello. The 365GT4 part of the new model's designation was familiar enough to any Ferrari buff, in representing a grand tourer with a total capacity of 4390cc and four overhead camshafts. As a model number it wasn't so different from the official title of the car it was set to replace, the much-loved Daytona, the 365GTB/4. Yet similar as the labels superficially seemed, the two cars could hardly have been more different.

The B in the Daytona's case stood for Berlinetta, and one of the Bs on the BB stood for Berlinetta too, but the other was the first appearance for a brand-new designation for Ferrari road cars – B for Boxer; just one little letter signifying the change from the classic V12 layout which Ferrari had embraced for so long, to a flat-12 layout in which the pistons moved in horizontal opposition.

And that was only half the story of the great leap from Daytona to BB. The new car was mid-engined too, the first 'full-sized' roadgoing Ferrari ever to adopt the theoretically ideally balanced layout of mechanical elements, even though it had already been *de rigueur* for many years on the race circuit; even though Ferrari had already proved its efficacy for the road, with the excellent smaller Dinos; even though his increasingly worrying and utterly determined rival from Sant'Agata Bolognese had had a mid-engined supercar in his catalogue for over six years and wasn't prepared to ease the pressure.

Tradition dies hard at Ferrari though, and as Maranello's first 'full-size' mid-engined road car the 365GT4/BB could hardly have failed to be controversial. Depending on your point of view and degree of conservatism, it was either Ferrari dragging themselves into the modern world or Ferrari breaking faith with the conventional wisdom that had served so well for so long. More than one magazine pitted the new Berlinetta Boxer against the old Daytona, and not all were totally convinced that the new car was actually a *better* car, but that's the way of the world.

Part of the problem, of course, was that for all the desirability of fashion and modernity, Ferrari's front-engined line could hardly have been accused of going into decline; the Daytona was one of the most totally accomplished cars Ferrari had ever made, and some would argue the most accomplished front-engined supercar that *anyone* ever made. But the fact was that politically its time had come, because, wherever your loyalties lay, it was hard to deny that newcomer Lamborghini had stolen Ferrari's supercar thunder by launching the transverse-mid-engined Miura in 1966, while Ferrari had remained faithful to the front-engined ethos with the Daytona.

It certainly wasn't that Ferrari lacked the technical wherewithal. He had used mid-engines in racing since the early 1960s, and 'flat' engines on and off for almost ten years. Most significant of all perhaps, in a company now far

Compared to Lamborghini's sensational Miura and the stunning Countach, Ferrari's first big mid-engined car looked almost plain (far left) and details like the engine cover (below) were rather bitty. Anti-glare materials gave the interior (left) a functional look.

more dedicated to commercial success than its founder had originally envisaged, both the Formula 1 and prototype sports racers had mid-mounted, flat-12 engines, and commercially it was, as ever, politic for Ferrari road cars to reflect Ferrari racing cars.

Lamborghini, on the other hand, had never raced at all, but had managed to threaten Ferrari's road car supremacy nonetheless, through innovation versus conservatism. Yet still it came as a surprise to some of the Ferrari faithful when Ferrari made the mid-engined move.

At least by the time the car was officially on sale, they had had a while to get used to the idea, because the BB concept was first shown as early as 1971 at the Turin Show. They also had a new incentive to accept change, because Lamborghini had already shown off the sensational prototype Countach.

Alongside that, the BB was almost staid, but it had all the great Ferrari virtues of race-bred design and superb engineering. The layout wasn't *quite* conventional. The classic mid-engine format usually implies an engine behind the driver but ahead of the gearbox and final drive and hence ahead of the rear wheels; the BB, giving due consideration to compact packaging, mounted the gearbox below the wide but shallow engine, the final drive behind, and the radiator in the front of the car, avoiding all the tack-on rear cooling vents that the Countach soon sprouted.

It was a good solution, avoiding any impression of aping Lamborghini and compromised only by the fact that it did set the centre of gravity of the engine and transmission a little higher than would have been ideal. The engine itself had the same dimensions as the Daytona's, which meant it was possible to use the same pistons and rods, but beyond that virtually everything else was new. Indeed, one feature of the engine was another first for Ferrari – toothed-belt drive for the four overhead camshafts. With two triple-choke Weber carburettors above each cylinder bank, the 4.4-litre engine produced 344bhp and 302lb ft of torque, both a little way short of the mighty Daytona's figures, and

The low and severely wedge-shaped nose (left and below) gave Ferrari and Pininfarina a problem that was to become familiar to builders of mid-engined cars trying to meet international regulations – accommodating the headlamps. Flip-ups were the answer.

Although the flat-12 engine was at the back (above) the radiator was at the front, which gave quite a bluff nose (opposite) and needed bonnet louvres (above left). The BB was a wide car (far left), but tightly packaged, especially at the tail.

365GT4/BB
SPECIFICATION

ENGINE
Flat-12

CAPACITY
4391cc

BORE x STROKE
81.0 x 71.0mm

COMPRESSION RATIO
8.8:1

POWER
344bhp

VALVE GEAR
Double overhead camshafts

FUEL SYSTEM
Four Weber 40IFC3 carburettors

TRANSMISSION
Five-speed manual

FRONT SUSPENSION
Independent, by double wishbones, coil springs, telescopic dampers

REAR SUSPENSION
Independent, by double wishbones, coil springs, telescopic dampers

BRAKES
All discs

WHEELS
Centre-lock alloy

WEIGHT
c.3800lb (1723kg)

MAXIMUM SPEED
c.175mph (281kph)

NUMBER MADE, DATES
c.387, 1973–6

the BB was surprisingly very little lighter than a Daytona.

The majority of the body (styled by Pininfarina, of course) was in steel, but with aluminium for the door skins, the bonnet and the engine cover – and the black lower panels used to emphasise the waistline were in glass fibre. It clothed a typical Ferrari tubular chassis (in this case fabricated mainly in square tubing), with independent suspension all round by unequal length wishbones and coil springs – the latter doubled up at the rear, which naturally carried a fairly marked weight bias.

Popular prejudices aside, the Boxer was a success. It wasn't quite such a practical Grand Tourer as the Daytona, partly for lack of luggage space, partly because of proximity of mid-engine to occupants' ears, but it was as quick or quicker on top speed and very little adrift in terms of acceleration. It was also a little lighter to drive, with exceptional roadholding and handling but a slightly less forgiving nature towards its final limits, typical of a mid-engined car.

In initial form it still didn't sell in great numbers, something less than 400 in almost four years, but it did put

Ferrari back in the running against the Countach. So, having established that the formula actually worked, Ferrari uprated the Boxer engine in 1976 via a slightly bigger bore and markedly longer stroke, to 4942cc, 360bhp and 332lb ft of torque. It also gained dry-sump lubrication, a stronger clutch and revised gearing.

As the 512BB, the 5-litre model reverted to the old numbering system. Visually it changed very little save for small rear-brake cooling ducts, a deeper nose (to improve aerodynamic balance) and a slightly longer, broader tail, covering wider rear tyres; in character it changed quite markedly, with a more powerful yet lower revving engine giving a rather more flexible nature, if not any greater outright performance, while making it easier for Ferrari to meet tougher emissions legislation. That was also the spur for the final revision of the Boxer, late in 1981 when, as the 512BBi, it adopted Bosch fuel injection and sacrificed some 20bhp to stay clean.

In 1984, the first big mid-engined Ferrari gave way to the second, the Testarossa, and, as usual, there were those who lamented the progress.

TESTAROSSA

Through much of the 1970s Ferrari had a major problem, a technical problem at root, but one which manifested itself as the worst kind of commercial problem. From 1973 to 1984, Ferrari's flagship supercar had been the Berlinetta Boxer in all its various forms, but Ferrari had never been able officially to sell the Boxers in the large and lucrative American market.

That's not to say that no Boxers found their way to the USA; they did, but as individual and independent imports which had to suffer varying degrees of power-sapping modification to meet the swingeing environmental protection laws that increasingly shaped the US market.

Ferrari, it must be said, had put himself into that situation quite consciously. Even as the Boxer was being conceived, US Federal laws were becoming tougher but, as ever, Ferrari's stubborn autonomy left little room for compromise – either on emasculated low-emission engines or for impact-absorbing bodywork addenda. Instead he simply adopted the attitude that if the Americans couldn't buy their supercars unfettered, they wouldn't bother buying them at all, so he would just carry on supplying the easier-to-adapt V8 models and keep the unsullied twelve-cylinder cars for the Europeans who truly appreciated them.

Eventually, of course, even that was a little harder to reconcile, but although Ferrari could respond to increasingly strict European emissions laws in 1977 by replacing the original 4.4-litre Boxer with the full 5-litre 512, and in 1981 by swapping the Weber carburation for Bosch injection, he still wouldn't make concessions to US standards.

As the 1980s approached, it was a stubbornness he could ill afford. The fact is that more exotic cars are more expensive cars and more expensive cars promise bigger profits than more mundane ones, even V8 Ferraris. On the other hand, even in improving the Boxer's social conscience and refinement as far as Europe demanded, Ferrari had also rather clipped its wings, and the new car wasn't quite so quick as the old; in reality, it *couldn't* retrospectively be made to work in original form for America. By his earlier reckoning that didn't matter but, unfortunately, Lamborghini for one had proved that the US supercar market, legislation or no, was far from evaporating.

So in 1978 Ferrari bit the bullet and commissioned Pininfarina to start thinking about a new generation twelve-cylinder flagship, based on the Boxer philosophy but pandering to the New World again. Later, he could

console his pride with the no-holds-barred 288GTO, but for the moment he would show that he could not only meet the legislators, but also offer a Ferrari with refinement – a car of superlative performance that was also user-friendly. More of a true GT car, he might say.

Being Ferrari, though, he wasn't going to cop out. Yes, the new car should be legally and socially acceptable, easier to drive, better equipped, more comfortable, even with the luggage space the Boxers had always lacked. More practical in fact; but it also had to be quicker and better handling,

The absence of cooling vents on the nose (far left) hints that although the front has a dramatic grille, the two radiators are actually in the rear haunches, fed by the distinctive straked side vents. Engine and occupants can now both stay cool.

with better brakes and less tendency to aerodynamic lift.

One of the main user criticisms of the Boxers quickly set a major new parameter. A front radiator with pipes running alongside the cockpit to the mid engine had always made the BBs prone to being uncomfortably hot; the new car would move its cooling, Formula 1-style, to the rear, with twin radiators just aft of the doors. That would not only solve the comfort problem but would also improve the weight distribution (and reduce the 'dumbell' handling effect by moving weight from end to middle), it would help create some more luggage space under the nose, and it would make best use of the wider rear end coincidentally envisaged to accommodate wider rear tyres.

In the event, after Pininfarina had developed the shape in their full-scale wind tunnel, the necessary air intakes for the rear radiators would also give the new car the most distinctive part of its look – the deep side ducts punctuated by their five body-coloured strakes. At first they weren't universally popular, and were seen as being rather gimmicky for a Ferrari, but in fact they weren't just a styling trick; they direct the airflow very precisely and they answered a legislative problem requiring a grill of sorts for such a large side opening.

Behind them and the new radiators was a much revised version of the all-aluminium, four-camshaft, flat-12 engine of the earlier Boxers. Its basic architecture and near 5-litre capacity were similar to that of the 512, but it made a major leap in adapting four-valve cylinder heads, for both power and drivability. It came further up to date with electro-mechanical Bosch KE-Jetronic fuel injection instead of the purely mechanical K-Jetronic, and with Magnetti Marelli Microplex electronic programmed ignition.

The Testarossa is a big car (right), but strictly a two-seater (above). Ferrari specifically wanted it to be more user-friendly than the BB, with higher standards of interior trim and equipment and lighter controls.

The redesign trimmed some 44lb (20kg) from the weight of the engine while claimed outputs gained 50bhp, to 390bhp at 5300rpm, and 29lb ft of torque, to 362lb ft at 4500rpm. As before, the engine sits above the gearbox and final drive, sparing Ferrari the option of following either the transverse layout of Lamborghini's Miura or the 'back-to-front' configuration of the Countach.

The red-crackle-painted cam covers and red ribbed panels on the intake plenums both contributed to the new car's name, Testarossa – literally translatable as Redhead. As with the GTO, it was not a name that Ferrari used lightly; it was a great name in Ferrari history through the racing Testa Rossas of the late 1950s and early 1960s, but was now used for the first time on a Ferrari road car.

At a stroke the new model achieved virtually all it set out to achieve. While meeting all appropriate US legislation, it reinstated full 180mph (289kph) performance, with 0–60mph (97kph) in around 5.8 seconds, 0–100mph (161kph) in 12.7 seconds, and the sort of flexibility that made it a truly practical supercar. Its tubular steel chassis with steel monocoque centre section was based closely on the 512 chassis, with the same wishbone and coil-spring suspension all-round, but the Testarossa sits on a longer wheelbase and wider tracks, considerably wider at the rear. That combines with more rubber on the road to give the Testarossa better grip, and with the redistributed weight to give more predictable handling than the Boxer. It's still tail heavy, and it's a little softer in deference to a more comfortable ride, but it's very well behaved – more agile than its size might suggest, flattering for an average driver, very rewarding for a competent and enthusiastic one. Bigger brakes (now with 12-inch (300mm) diameter ventilated discs and four-piston calipers) were added to match

the improved performance, and a bigger twin-plate clutch not only copes with the additional power but also allows a lighter action.

That too was part of the programme to make the Testarossa as refined and civilised as could be for such a quick two-seater. Compared to the Boxer's, the cockpit is bigger and better equipped, and there's more luggage space both behind the seats and under the bonnet. There are niceties like a height-adjustable steering column, electrically adjustable seats and, of course, standard air-conditioning such as you would expect in any other luxury car, for that's what the Testarossa became as well as being a performance car. It is all set to carry on well into the 1990s, possibly with four-wheel drive and other technical sophistications to come. If it's the long-term future face of Ferraris for the road, it's not a bad one . . .

The strakes in the side vents (far left) not only disguise the size of the cooling openings but direct airflow and satisfy legal requirements.

The Testarossa has a distinct arrow-head shape, which widens dramatically at the rear (above and below) and is emphasised by light layout.

TESTAROSSA SPECIFICATION

ENGINE
Flat-12

CAPACITY
4942cc

BORE x STROKE
82.0 x 78.0mm

COMPRESSION RATIO
9.2:1

POWER
390bhp

VALVE GEAR
Double overhead camshafts, four valves per cylinder

FUEL SYSTEM
Bosch K-Jetronic injection

TRANSMISSION
Five-speed manual

FRONT SUSPENSION
Independent, by double wishbones, coil springs, telescopic dampers

REAR SUSPENSION
Independent, by double wishbones, coil springs, telescopic dampers

BRAKES
All discs

WHEELS
Centre-lock alloy

WEIGHT
c.4000lb (1814kg)

MAXIMUM SPEED
c.180mph (289kph)

NUMBER MADE, DATES
1984–1991;
1991–1994 512TR;
1994–1996 512M

288GTO

Standing for *Gran Turismo Omologato*, GTO is not a designation that Enzo Ferrari used lightly. The first time it appeared was on the all-conquering 1963 250GTO and its siblings up to 1964, the second was on this, the 1984 288GTO. In between, Ferrari had had GTs and LMs, GTBs and GTCs and GTSs, Ps and Ms and Dinos and Daytonas, but never another GTO.

Introducing the hallowed letters again at the 1984 Geneva Show was an emotive move, but it was a perfectly legitimate one too. Exactly as with the 1960s legend, the *Omologato* part of the title signified what the original intention for the car was – racing homologation, to which end just enough examples were to be built to satisfy the FIA's prevailing requirements. In the 1960s, the run of 250GTOs stretched to just thirty-nine cars; in the case of the 288, Ferrari would need to build 200 examples, to make the car eligible for the new Group B GT category.

It had taken something out of the ordinary to tempt Ferrari back towards an involvement in sports car racing, a discipline the works had given up in 1973 to concentrate solely on Grands Prix. Having won so much over the years in the sports racing categories however, and well aware of the commercial spin-off in doing so again, Ferrari had

obviously kept an eye on the possibilities for a return. Unfortunately, through the rest of the 1970s and well into the 1980s the regulations had favoured purpose-built sports racing machinery and left little scope for such production-based models as Ferrari could have fielded; and Ferrari were in no position to divert resources, financial or technical, from their often uphill struggle to stay consistently competitive in Grand Prix racing.

And then along came Group B, a class which the FIA intended to open up the increasingly specialised and expensive sports car classes to more mainstream manufacturers, not just for racing but for rallying too, and the cars would essentially have to be at least theoretically usable on the road. Finally, there would be that homologation requirement, for a minimum run of 200 cars, so any interested manufacturer clearly would have to sell a majority of output, however expensively, as road cars.

For Ferrari it was the irresistible bait, at once an opportunity to get back into high profile events such as Le Mans with a serious chance of success (albeit probably through private customers), and to sell a goodly number of highly profitable road cars. The car to match all those criteria would be another *Gran Turismo Omologato*.

Seen from above, the 288GTO has a distinct 'Coke-bottle' outline (below), emphasising its '328-on-steroids' look. Pop-up lights (right) are penalty of a low nose line.

Although the GTO is bigger all round than the 328, with long wheelbase and markedly wider front and rear tracks, it has the same beautiful proportions (overleaf), showing that Pininfarina could make a racing car just as elegant as a road car.

C224 EUL

Compared to the later F40, and to almost any vaguely comparable car from another manufacturer, the GTO was admirably free from tack-on aerodynamic aids, save the small kick-up lip on the trailing edge of the tail and the inevitable extra cooling vents (opposite page and far left). One major difference from the 328 was longitudinal rather than transverse engine location (left) with the transaxle behind the block rather than in the sump – giving both better balance and better accessibility for the car's originally-planned but never fulfilled racing role.

On the surface, the 1980s GTO might seem to be nothing much more than a pumped-up 328, but that is far from doing it justice. The Pininfarina-penned lines are 328-like, certainly, but little else was so mundane. For one thing, the wheelbase of its multi-tubular steel chassis was around 4½ inches longer than a 328's and both front and rear tracks were substantially wider. Under the skin, the V8 engine was mounted longitudinally rather than transversely, ahead of a new ZF five-speed transaxle with limited-slip differential, in place of the gearbox-under-block arrangement of the 328. For a racing model, given the longer wheelbase, that gave a number of advantages, including more space, a lower centre of gravity and better accessibility.

The engine itself might not have a dozen cylinders, but it was Ferrari's most potent ever for a road car when it was launched, and second only to the F40 even now. Capacity, as the type number suggests, was 2.8 litres, from eight cylinders with attractively large bores and short stroke, giving space for four valves per cylinder and an ability to rev happily to a 7700rpm redline.

That in itself wasn't enough to give Ferrari the sort of power that would be needed if the GTO was to go racing, but add two Japanese-made IHI turbochargers, each with its own intercooler, and you have a different story. On that basis, the FIA regulations required that Ferrari multiply the actual capacity by an equivalency factor of 1.4, nominally putting the turbocharged 2855cc GTO just inside the 4-litre normally aspirated limit. With maximum boost of 11.6psi, governed by a single wastegate behind the engine and between the two banks of the Weber-Marelli injection system, the 288 produced 400bhp and 366lb ft of torque for the road and promised 600bhp or more in racing spec.

The other part of the racing equation is to throw away weight, and Ferrari did that with the 288GTO largely by the use of many of the exotic lightweight materials that thus far he had only used in his Grand Prix cars. The main shell was in a glass fibre composite, the bonnet and complete rear engine cover in Kevlar and the interior bulkheads used a mixture of Kevlar, fire resistant Nomex and aluminium honeycomb. The door skins used humble aluminium. Even in fully-equipped road trim, the GTO was claimed to weigh only 2700lb (1224kg), around 300lb (136kg) *lighter* than the smaller 328.

That gave a power to weight ratio in the region of 330bhp per ton even in road trim, and the impressively wide torque spread (with more than 300lb ft from 2500rpm and the peak at a lowish 3800) gave immense flexibility. At 4000rpm it was already developing 300bhp. In spite of the use of two small turbos rather than one big one, there was a fair amount of turbo lag at low revs, but beyond around 2000rpm that rapidly decreased, and beyond 3500rpm on full boost the acceleration was breathtaking. The GTO would reach 60mph (97kph) in around 4.8 seconds, 100mph (161kph) in just over 10 seconds. Gear ratios were also superbly spaced, offering 58, 93, 130 and 166mph (93, 149, 209 and 267kph respectively) in the first four and a claimed 189mph (304kph) in fifth. It was the fastest road car Ferrari had made.

Much of the appeal of the GTO, though, was in how remarkably compact and road-usable it was for a car with such prodigious power and performance. Yes, it had a good deal of extra rubber on the road, and some newly bulging arches to cover it, but it still felt hardly bigger than the diminutive 328. It was also a highly civilised car inside, fully trimmed and nicely finished, in stark contrast to the F40 which eventually eclipsed it as the fastest roadgoing Ferrari of all.

Finally, of course, it had the roadholding and stopping power to match, with the usual double wishbones and coil springs all round (rubber bushed on the road cars for comfort) and ventilated disc brakes of more than a foot diameter inside the 16-inch split-rim wheels, in classic Ferrari five-spoke competition pattern.

The fact that the 1980s GTO never had the opportunity to show that it could live up to the racing heritage of the 1960s GTO was more a sign of the times than a sign of Ferrari's ability to build the right car. The company easily built and sold the requisite 200, and the 288GTO was almost immediately elevated to the status of small-volume classic, but it never had a proper racing career. In rallying in particular, Group B was proving faster and far more dangerous than the FIA had ever envisaged, as manufacturers like Audi, Lancia, Ford and Peugeot ploughed in vast financial and technical resources. On the circuits, the GTO's main rival might have been the Porsche 959, but the showdown never really came. After a series of horrific rallying accidents, the FIA pulled the plug on Group B in 1986 and Ferrari's sports racing comeback was sadly nipped in the bud.

288GTO SPECIFICATION

ENGINE
90° V8, turbocharged

CAPACITY
2855cc

BORE x STROKE
80.0 × 71.0mm

COMPRESSION RATIO
7.6:1

POWER
400bhp

VALVE GEAR
Double overhead camshafts, four valves per cylinder

FUEL SYSTEM
Weber-Marelli injection, two IHI turbochargers

TRANSMISSION
Five-speed manual

FRONT SUSPENSION
Independent, by double wishbones, coil springs, telescopic dampers

REAR SUSPENSION
Independent, by double wishbones, coil springs, telescopic dampers

BRAKES
All discs

WHEELS
Centre-lock alloy

WEIGHT
c.2700lb (1224kg)

MAXIMUM SPEED
c.189mph (304kph)

NUMBER MADE, DATES
269, 1984-5

F40

In 1987, in his 90th year, Enzo Ferrari would celebrate 40 years as a car builder under his own name. Never having been a man burdened with undue modesty and, perhaps knowing that it must be the last major anniversary he would see, Ferrari planned to celebrate in style.

He had every right; he could look back on a history of eight Formula 1 manufacturer's championships, ten driver's championships, approaching 100 Grands Prix wins, nine Le Mans wins and thousands of other triumphs. He could look back on such classic road cars as the first 166s, the 250 dynasty, the Daytona, the Dino and the Testarossa. Although his empire was now owned by Fiat, Ferrari would still make his own statement – in his own words, 'the best Ferrari ever'. So the car to commemorate his first 40 years had to be something special, and it was: the F40.

Significantly, the last car that Ferrari himself would ever launch would be very much like the first, in bridging the gap between road car and racing car – handsomely aggressive in its functionally-styled clothing, uncompromisingly fearsome in its state-of-the-art technical specification. Ferrari unveiled it personally, and with typical bravura, in front of a small band of invited journalists and personalities in Maranello in July 1987. As the red cover was drawn back, it was instantly apparent that the ultimate supercar honours were back with the Prancing Horse.

The F40 was introduced as the fastest roadgoing car ever built; as simple as that, with no need for qualifications. Its claimed top speed of 323kph equates to 201mph, the first time a road car had bettered 200; it would accelerate to 60mph (97kph) in 3.5 seconds, or to twice that speed in just 11.5 seconds. Only Porsche's ultra-high-tech 959 could offer any serious challenge to those numbers, but not to the new Ferrari's aura, because the F40 also promised an awesome singularity of purpose that the Porsche, for all its performance, just couldn't match.

Stuttgart's supercar, after all, had the softening sophistication of electronically-controlled four-wheel drive, automatically-variable ride-height and damping programmes, a clever six-speed gearbox, the pampering interior luxuries of leather, hi-fi and air conditioning; Maranello's supercar had only the basic race-car engineering of sledgehammer power, rear-wheel drive and minimal weight, without even anti-lock braking. And where the 959 had the softly-moulded good looks of the familiar 911 family, the F40, with its massive scoops and wings, its aggressive angularity,

The aerodynamic purity of the F40 (left) is as important as sheer power in making it one of the fastest cars in the world yet without sacrificing real-road stability. The embossed F40 logo in the rear spoiler (above) gives away the car's composite body material.

Fast and aggressive as it is (right) the F40 is fully road legal, which demands the usual attention to lighting laws (above) and even full rear view mirrors.

had just the wildly uncompromising look of a real racer.

It was appropriate that the F40 should be styled by Pininfarina, the house which had handled the vast majority of Ferraris since the early 1950s. Form followed function; the high rear wing and deep front spoiler help nail the car to the ground at maximum speed, the scattered ducts feed radiators and intercoolers, brakes and engine bay. Even the louvred rear plexiglass window is playing its part, and if the drag coefficient is a mere 0.34Cd, that's the price for keeping a 200mph supercar on the ground and off the boil.

The body is largely in plastics and composites, for lightness. Each skeletal door, for example, weighs only 3.3lb (1.5kg). The Kevlar-covered sills are deep and wide, unselfconsciously naked as a styling touch to rub in the competition-bred image of the beast. The whole cockpit serves to do that. The seats are high-backed racing buckets trimmed in red velour over Kevlar shells, pierced near the high shoulder supports and down by the hips to accommodate the belts. They adjust for reach but not for height or rake, and the chunky three-spoke Momo steering wheel is steadfastly fixed. There's little creature comfort here. The only real trim is a basic grey cloth over the dash, centre tunnel and front 'screen pillars. There are no niceties like carpets, electric windows, central locking, or internally adjustable mirrors, not even proper door handles, just cord

pulls. There *is* rudimentary air conditioning, but only to keep the driver from being parboiled in the spartan cockpit. You can pay your autostrada tolls through a hinged flap in the plastic side windows; the kerb weight of the car is only just over one ton, about 1100kg.

New chassis technology kept the weight down. The basics are a welded steel spaceframe, but the usual sheetmetal panelling and box structures are also largely replaced by modern composites like Kevlar and carbon fibre, bonded on in finest aerospace fashion. The chassis is thus some 20 per cent lighter than the best conventional equivalent, and as much as three times stiffer. It isn't yet a technique that could be transferred to mass production, but then Ferrari never intended to build more than a few hundred of his ultimate supercar.

The suspension is by unequal length wishbones and coil springs, all round, with adjustable Koni dampers and substantial anti-roll bars. The brakes, grabbed by four-piston calipers, are huge Brembo discs, 13 inches (330mm) across, ventilated and cross drilled, with iron faces sand-wiching light alloy cores to reduce unsprung weight. The brakes nestle inside 17-inch (430mm) diameter wheels, 10 inches (255mm) wide at the front and no less than 13 inches wide at the rear, shod with Pirelli P-Zero tyres of 245/40 and 335/35 section. It is all very akin to racing technology.

The F40's engine was at the time of its launch the most powerful ever offered for a road car. Derived from that of the 1984 288GTO, it's a short-stroke 2936cc V8 with twin Japanese-made IHI turbochargers, four overhead camshafts, thirty-two valves and dry-sump lubrication. It's a bit bigger than the GTO's unit, more oversquare, with a new crankshaft, better lubrication and more boost. In road trim, with F1-derived state-of-the-art Weber-Marelli injection

and ignition management, the F40's engine produces 478bhp and 425lb ft of torque.

With the F40's lightness that equates to around 450bhp per ton, and potentially fearsome performance. This is where the F40 differs most of all from any rival, which at launch time meant only the 959 but which might now nominally include the 492bhp, 202mph (325kph) Lamborghini Diablo. The others wrap their performance in a velvet glove; the Ferrari is a bare-knuckle car.

It demands both effort and skill from the driver; the controls are heavy, from unassisted steering to massive brakes; and controlling 478bhp in so little weight requires a deft touch. There is little by way of subtlety, the bare cabin resonates to the cacophony of the engine, the rear-ward view is mostly of bodywork and cooling vents, the seats keep you pinned precisely in place. Certainly it's possible to drive the F40 gently; up to a point it is docile and always tractable, but press it at all hard and it is rabid. The big tyres offer a phenomenal amount of grip and the stiff chassis and race-bred suspension give faultless precision, but there is always the power to hurl the F40 into lurid oversteer, or to light the back tyres and leave molten black lines on even a dry road. By 3900rpm more than 300bhp are already being unleashed, by 5000rpm it's more than 400, and between 3000 and 3500rpm the torque curve explodes almost vertically towards its peak. Such power is way outside normal realms, even for many an experienced test driver, but it is the total lack of compromise that impresses most people most.

Of course, it's exactly what Ferrari intended, probably the last of the great 'pre-electronic' mid-engined supercars in just the same way that the Daytona before it was the last of the mighty front-engined classics. It's a fitting memorial.

F40
SPECIFICATION

ENGINE
90° V8, turbocharged

CAPACITY
2936cc

BORE x STROKE
82.0 × 69.5mm

COMPRESSION RATIO
7.7:1

POWER
478bhp

VALVE GEAR
Double overhead camshafts, four valves per cylinder

FUEL SYSTEM
Weber-Marelli injection, two IHI turbochargers

TRANSMISSION
Five-speed manual

FRONT SUSPENSION
Independent, by double wishbones, coil springs, telescopic dampers

REAR SUSPENSION
Independent, by double wishbones, coil springs, telescopic dampers

BRAKES
All discs

WHEELS
Centre-lock alloy

WEIGHT
c.2400lb (1088kg)

MAXIMUM SPEED
c.201mph (323kph)

NUMBER MADE, DATES
1989–1994

348

Every Ferrari ever built, save perhaps the first one, could be said to have had a hard act to follow. Howsoever any new model is greeted at its introduction (and that hasn't always been with open arms), you can pretty well guarantee that by the time it comes to be replaced it will be loved and revered, while the newcomer is seen as just another nail in the coffin of Ferrari tradition. And when that newcomer in its turn comes to be replaced, *it* will be loved and revered, and so on, ad infinitum.

The first Ferrari for the 1990s, the 348, is no exception. When it superseded the voluptuous 328 late in 1989, there were those who thought it was mundane, those who were offended by the stylist's need for a dummy front grille even though the radiator had now moved to the back, those, inevitably, who thought it just didn't have the Ferrari *spirit* anymore. But they soon came round.

A couple of rungs down from the ultra-spectacular but strictly limited-edition F40, and the sophisticated twelve-cylinder glamour of the expensive Testarossa, the eight-cylinder 'entry-level' Ferrari might look to be something of a poor relation but in reality it is anything but.

The 348 is the latest example of what *really* keeps Ferrari in business, the bread and butter model that pays for the jam. Far from being a mere sideline for Ferrari's engineers to dash off between designing the big stuff, these are cars that have to be absolutely right. These are the cars that have to satisfy a much wider audience, the ones bought by the customers to whom money frequently *is* some option. And this is one sector where the competition grows tougher day by day: Porsches have long been a traditional enemy, now the Japanese are coming onto the scene too, with cars like the highly acclaimed (and by Ferrari standards almost bargain basement) Honda NSX. Where Honda have led, the other front-line Japanese car makers are already lining up to follow. In the junior supercar stakes, just being a Ferrari is no longer enough.

The 348, though, has one thing going for it that the Japanese, however good they are technically, don't have; it has the Ferrari bloodline. The 348 is a lineal descendant of the 328 and 308 dynasty, and via those models back, in spirit at least, to the Dinos that started the smaller Ferrari line back in the late 1960s. First there was the 206 in 1968, then the 246 from 1969. The V8 family started with the misunderstood Bertone-styled 2+2 Dino 308GT4 in

In continuing the theme of the 'smaller' Ferraris growing steadily bigger and more mature, the 348 (below) introduced a softer, more rounded look, adding styling touches like the slatted rear end (left) to emphasise family ties with the Testarossa. Some 'changes don't change though (above).

1974, then got into its stride properly with the 308GTB in 1975 and its spyder sibling, the GTS, from 1977. In 1980 the line split to complement the strictly two-seater GTBs and GTSs with the squarer-edged 2+2 Mondials – a much more readily accepted car than the unfortunate 308GT4. In 1982 along came more power and more refinement in the shape of the four-valve-per-cylinder *quattrovalvole* upgrade of the 3-litre V8, and then in 1985 the whole family grew to 3.2 litres, with the 328GTB and GTS and the 3.2 Mondials in both coupé and Cabrio form.

Most recently of all, late in 1989, the Mondials were given a new 3.4-litre version of the faithful V8, and a new model, the 348, replaced the 328; its replacement came amid the usual cries of 'shame'.

More readily than most the 348 gained acceptance, even acclaim, as the sceptics realised what a leap forward it actually is. It's no simple rehash of the 328; it's to all intents and purposes a completely new car. It's more grown up, more sophisticated, more socially accomplished

perhaps; just the thing to hold its own in the new generation, where performance is nowadays perhaps taken for granted and the packaging and refinement that accompany it can tip the sales scales.

It isn't just its new Pininfarina looks that are so smooth and genteel, the car's whole nature has changed. Apart from being an inch shorter overall, it is bigger. It sits on a 4-inch longer wheelbase (101mm) and it is no less than 7 inches (177mm) wider than the 328, with wider wheels and tyres and wider track too. With its chunky squareness and Testarossa-like side-strakes, it looks more Mondial than 328, but where the Mondial is a 2+2 the 348 is strictly in the two-seater-only tradition. It's moved a bit more up-market inside than its forebears, largely making use of the additional width. The seats are deeper and more shapely than of old, and with more widely spaced pedals with less offset the 348 is a more comfortable car for the (if a Ferrari allows one) average driver.

There's more of a production-line feel inside too, with an

Although the Ferrari legend was built on V12s, high-tech V8s such as the 348's fuel-injected, electronically-managed engine (top left) are fundamental to Ferrari's modern expansion. The purists will usually find something to criticise, like the 348's dummy grille (above left), but even the most cynical can't deny Pininfarina's touch (above).

integrated, sculpted line to the trim, and although most of the switchgear still comes from humbler Fiats the overall look is much less 'bitsa'. But the good news is that you will still not mistake the 348 for anything but a Ferrari; not just because of the familiar six-fingered metal gate for the slim chrome gearlever, nor just for the distinctive and comprehensive instruments, or the Prancing Horse in the centre of the steering wheel, but more for an indefinable aura of solidity and purposefulness. Nor is there any concession to the wrong kind of modern complexity. The 348 offers anti-lock brakes, but that's about all – there is no power assistance to take the edge from the steering feel; there are no electronic gizmos to stop the driver indulging the balance between power and grip. No frills.

And if any doubts remained at all, you need only start the engine. As suggested by the modern numbering system, the 348's is a 3.4-litre V8. It is a natural extension of the 308 and 328 line, a *quattrovalvole*, naturally, with four belt-driven overhead camshafts operating its four valves per cylinder. It sounds and feels like a Ferrari thoroughbred. It *is* a Ferrari thoroughbred.

It has gained a bit in both bore and stroke and a lot more in flexibility than even the added capacity suggests, largely thanks to more modern induction tract design. Ferrari claim a nice round 300bhp and 238lb ft of torque, so the junior league supercar isn't so junior any more.

More significant than the extra power is a complete rethinking of the power-train layout and the chassis construction. Where the 328 (and the Mondial) had a transverse engine with the gearbox mounted below, the 348 has reverted to a longitudinal engine, but keeping the overall length down by using a transverse gearbox, drawing on Grand Prix technology. This way the engine is mounted much lower than in the 328 and the whole car is better balanced. The chassis is no longer the traditional multi-tube affair but an easier-to-build amalgam of fabricated sections, more along the lines of a modern mass-produced monocoque and clothed in a mixture of steel and alumi-

nium, just as ever was. No cause for complaint even from the traditionalists, though, because the new structure provides a better than 50 per cent more rigid platform for the familiar coil-spring and wishbone suspension, and that is the basis for fine and consistent handling with a ride that's still taut and firm but acceptable to a 1990s Ferrari driver flattered by modern expectations.

This is the first face of Ferrari after Ferrari; Ferrari's bridge to the future. It might well have become a little softer and more sophisticated, but then the 166 Inters of 1948 were a bit softer and more sophisticated than the 166MM weren't they, and the 195s were a step forward from the 166s. Conservative or not, Ferrari only survives through progress, but there's nothing to say that progress has to mean the end of character. Drive an NSX, for instance, and you will know that you have driven the state of the art; but drive a 348 and you will know that you have driven a Ferrari. That's still what makes the difference.

Smooth and simple are the 1990s styling cues – as in the unobtrusive rear-window air vents and flush filler cap cover (far left). The interior has a more modern look too (below), but you could never forget this is a real Ferrari (right).

**348
SPECIFICATION**

ENGINE
90° V8

CAPACITY
3405cc

BORE x STROKE
85.0 x 75.0mm

COMPRESSION RATIO
10.4:1

POWER
300bhp

VALVE GEAR
Double overhead camshafts, four valves per cylinder

FUEL SYSTEM
Bosch Motronic 2.5 injection

TRANSMISSION
Five-speed manual

FRONT SUSPENSION
Independent, by double wishbones, coil springs, telescopic dampers

REAR SUSPENSION
Independent, by double wishbones, coil springs, telescopic dampers

BRAKES
All discs

WHEELS
Five-stud alloy

WEIGHT
c.3200lb (1451kg)

MAXIMUM SPEED
c.165mph (265kph)

NUMBER MADE, DATES
1988–1992, 1311

F355

Critics rarely have a bad word to say about a Ferrari when it is still on sale, but a second opinion, in later years, is often illuminating. Thus it was that everyone fawned over the 348tb of 1989 – 1994, but complained about its on-the-limit handling in later years.

Its successor, the F355, which arrived in 1994, had a difficult job. Not only would it have to be a successful 'entry-level' Ferrari (if such a description is even justified), but it was expected to be an improvement on the 348tb which it would replace.

Free of inter-company rivalries (which had been rife at the end of the 1980s, when Enzo Ferrari finally died), Maranello's engineers must have done the trick, for *Autocar*'s testers summarised their relief like this:

'Anyone who ever attempted to drive a 348 hard over a good road, or around a circuit, and scared themselves, will revel in what Ferrari has achieved with the F355.

'It is not simply a better-handling car, it is a different car, period; different manners, different limits, different *feel*. So much so that is now possible to venture deep into the abilities of the chassis and, in the right circumstances, go safely beyond its limits, something you'd never try in a 348 unless you were certifiable...'

Starting from the basis of the 348's mid-engined chassis, which had to be retained for financial reasons, the team was allowed to modify, improve, or replace almost everything else. Compared with the 348, therefore, the engine was bigger and more powerful, the transmission new, the suspension re-worked and more predictable, the body style by Pininfarina totally fresh, and for the first time, the under-body aerodynamics were used to advantage on a Ferrari road car.

That was just the start, for it was in the detail, and in the development, that the satisfying became appealing, the very good sensational, and the pleasure in driving became true ecstacy. In every way (and in the next five years the sales figures would prove it) the F355 was a better car, a two-seater of which Ferrari was always extremely proud.

As always, with any new car from Maranello, the engine came first. Although it was still a 90-degree V8, and therefore still tenuously linked to the original 308GT4 Dinos' V8 engine of 1973, it had been improved in almost every respect. Not only had 2mm extra in the stroke given 3,496cc instead of 3,405cc, but peak power had leapt from 300bhp to an impressive 380bhp.

A 13 per cent improvement from a mere 2.5 per cent capacity increase meant that remarkable things had occurred under the skin. This was the first Ferrari road-car engine to have *five* valves per cylinder – three inlet and two exhaust, controlled by twin overhead camshafts per bank – which breathed deeply and efficiently. Allied to titanium conrods, the latest Bosch Motoronic 2.7 engine management system, butterfly throttle valves for each cylinder, and re-worked exhaust systems, this was a remarkable power unit by any standards.

To get the best from the chassis, therefore, it needed to be mated to an excellent transmission which was new, transversely-mounted, and with six forward speeds. This, allied to a lightened clutch and new fast-action synchronizer rings, made the F355 feel so much more like a racing car for the road than anyone could have hoped.

All this, of course, was hidden by a new Pininfarina body style, another sleek and seductive iteration of that company's classic mid-engine, two-seater coupé theme (as ever, a drop-top Spider would soon be added to the range). More rounded than the 348, with plain side-mounted air intakes instead of stylised strakes and, for the first time on a Ferrari like this, with a transverse rear spoiler, it was as

compact as it was beautiful, as unmistakeable as it was also typically Ferrari. It was under the car, however, where there was most body innovation, with a full length under-tray, that managed the high-speed airflow as never before.

Slowly, and at a welcome pace, Ferrari was also updating its interiors, for the F355 had a more up-market facia/instrument panel layout than ever, still with the familiar type of drilled aluminium foot pedals, but this time with a seven-slot, rather than six-slot 'gate' for gearchanging.

Many mechanical innovations, shared the direction of Ferrari's road-car thinking. The ex-348 structure had been stiffened by 30 per cent, which meant that wheel movements could be more precisely controlled. Front and rear wheel tracks had been widened to aid stability, magnesium alloy wheels were larger (18 in. diameter), and tyres were wider, though front and rear springs had been softened and anti-roll bars stiffened up.

Innovative suspension dampers were electronically controlled, their settings sensitive to driving methods, road speed, cornering loads, and to the intensity of use of brakes, steering loads and accelerator. Added to this was speed-sensitive, rack-and-pinion power-assisted steering

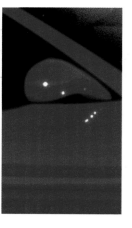

It was in the detail and in the development that the satisfying became appealing, the very good sensational, and the pleasure in driving became true ecstacy.

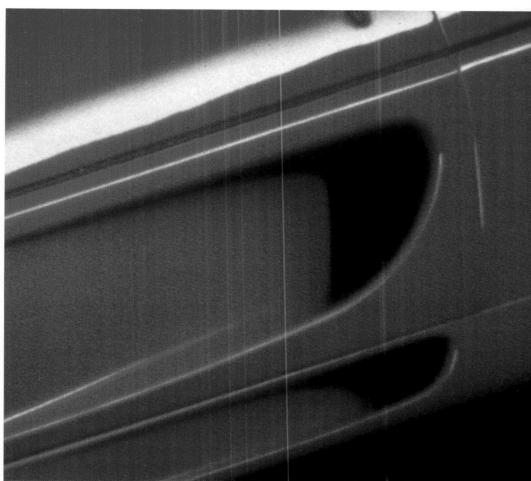

(the 348's steering had been purely manual), air-conditioning as standard, as was ABS braking, and one could see that Ferrari was at last reacting crisply to what its rivals from Germany and Japan had already standardised on their own cars.

As ever, though, it was the performance, and the manner of power delivery, which transcended all other features of the car. Although the F355's V8 would pull away gamely from 1,500 or 2,000rpm, it did not begin to show aural interest until 4,000rpm had been passed. Onwards and upwards, from that point the growl turned into a howl, rising in pitch to a scream, until a change was reluctantly made at 8,500rpm. More revs were available, but never needed, as alternative gear ratios could always be used!

By any standards, this was the best all-round mid-engined Ferrari road car yet made, which to F40 enthusiasts was an astonishing thing to admit. But at Ferrari nothing stands still, and it would only be five years before even better V8-engined machines were available.

F355
SPECIFICATION

ENGINE
90-deg V8

CAPACITY
3496cc

BORE X STROKE
85 x 77mm

COMPRESSION RATIO
11.1:1

POWER
380bhp

VALVE GEAR
Double overhead camshafts, five valves per cylinder

FUEL SYSTEM
Bosch Motronic engine management, and fuel injection

TRANSMISSION
Six-speed manual

FRONT SUSPENSION
Independent, by double wishbones, coil springs, electronic/telescopic dampers, anti-roll bar

REAR SUSPENSION
Independent, by double wishbones, coil springs, electronic/telescopic dampers, anti-roll bar

BRAKES
All discs

WHEELS
Five-stud alloy

WEIGHT
3194lb (1450kg)

MAXIMUM SPEED
173mph (278kph)

NUMBER MADE, DATES
11,000, produced 1994 – 1999

163

F50

Ferrari, it was said, would never be able to improve on the F40 of 1989. This car, crafted to commemorate Ferrari's fortieth anniversary, had been astonishingly fast, amazingly styled, and such a performance machine that it hardly seemed worth trying for improvements.

Yet Ferrari did – the result being the even more remarkable F50 of 1995. V12-engined where the F40 had been a V8, normally-aspirated where the F40 had been turbocharged, and more closely linked to F1 engineering than ever, it took limited-production indulgences to even greater heights. Not only that, but Ferrari was determined to make the F50 even more exclusive than the F40 had ever been – stating (and subsequently keeping to its promise) that no more than 349 cars would ever be produced. No fewer than 1,311 F40s had eventually been produced – which meant that an F50 would be almost four times more exclusive.

In 1990, when the project got under way, the brief was simple enough. Take the bare bones of the current Ferrari F1 single seater and convert it into the ultimate street-legal, two-seater road car.

The F50 took shape around a carbon fibre monocoque, clothed by a body shell in a mixture of carbon fibre, Kevlar and Nomex honeycomb. The engine was a detuned, though enlarged, version of the F1 car's five-valves-per-cylinder V12. Although air-conditioning was retained to keep hot-climate customers happy, many items usually regarded as standard were omitted – there was no power-assisted steering, anti-lock braking, or even a stereo/radio installation.

Not that any of the 349 customers (a figure which was quite swamped by those wanting to get their names on the build list...) seemed to complain. They would receive a two-seater capable of 200mph+ with a 4.7-litre V12-engine where exclusivity was guaranteed, where exceptional Pininfarina style was the envy of other motorists, and which could be run with a hard top in place, or left at home in the garage.

The F50, more than any previous Maranello model since perhaps the 250GTO of 1962, was sex-on-wheels, the epitome of gorgeous superiority and style. Some Ferraris could be practical, and others might be easier to drive but this was undoubtedly the ultimate in desirable cars. For those never likely to drive a Ferrari single seater, or even a racing sports car, the F50 was the next best thing.

Size for size, and dimension for dimension, the F50

The ultimate in desirable cars, the F50 was closely styled on the Ferrari F1 single seater to produce the ultimate street legal two-seater road car.

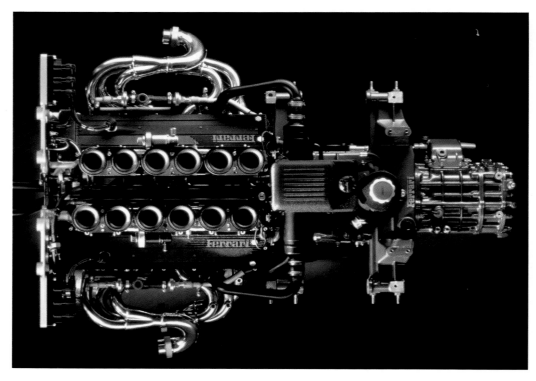

Where the F40's style had been all hard edges and planes, the F50 style was rounded and flowing. Most importantly, the F50 had a large capacity V12 engine, the layout of which went back to the very origins of Ferrari.

was just about the same size as the F40, though almost infinitely more costly and complex to produce. Where the F40's style had been all hard edges and planes, the F50 was rounded and flowing. Most importantly, the F50 had a large capacity V12 engine, the layout of which went back, viscerally, into the very origins of Ferrari.

F1 heritage? Truly there was no cheating here, for Ferrari actively set out to preserve as much of the current single-seater's legacy as possible. The fact that it took more than four years to bring the F50 to the market place merely confirms how long it takes *any* manufacturer to prepare to make cars in numbers.

The V12 was a de-tuned and enlarged version of the F1 car's 65-deg power unit, with a larger bore and stroke to ensure more torque, but with less extreme camshaft profiles, and steel (instead of pneumatic) valve springs to limit peak revs to 9,000rpm. This basic five-valve/twin-cam engine was certainly capable of more (out-and-out F1 engines peaked at 13,000rpm and more), but even at 520bhp it was

already the most powerful Ferrari of all time, and was quite strong enough to push the new car up to 200mph and beyond. Constructed from an intriguing cocktail of high-tech/aerospace materials, the F50's monocoque was the single major component which ensured that production would be at a very leisurely rate. Once moulded, the unit needed to be 'cured' for lengthy periods in a high-temperature autoclave or pressure oven, a process which took days rather than hours.

Every other major mechanical item – engine, transmission, suspension, steering and cooling systems – had to be fixed directly to the carbon fibre monocoque through light-alloy inserts which were bonded into place, so there was no room for compromise either in geometry and layout, or in the refinement of the assembly.

If there was noise, vibration, and some harshness, so be it. Although Ferrari spent thousands of hours in minimising this, they kept reminding themselves, and their customers, that this was F1 engineering which was being

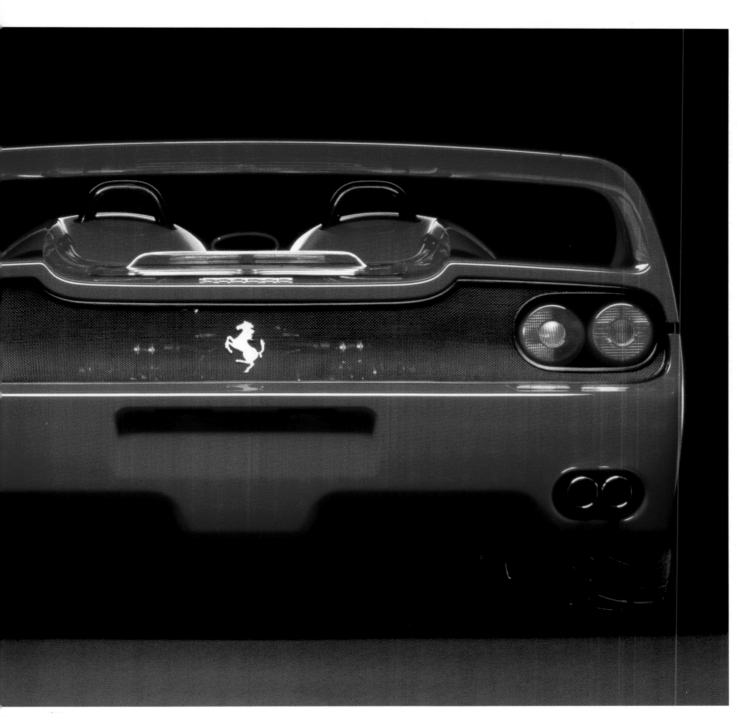

F50
SPECIFICATION

ENGINE
65–deg V12

CAPACITY
4698cc

BORE X STROKE
85 x 69mm

COMPRESSION RATIO
11.3:1

POWER
520bhp

VALVE GEAR
Double overhead camshafts,
five valves per cylinder

FUEL SYSTEM
Bosch Motronic engine
management, and fuel injection

TRANSMISSION
Six-speed manual

FRONT SUSPENSION
Independent, by double
wishbones, coil springs,
electronic/telescopic
dampers, anti-roll bar

REAR SUSPENSION
Independent, by double wishbones, coil springs, electronic/
telescopic dampers, anti-roll bar

BRAKES
All discs

WHEELS
Centre–lock alloy

WEIGHT
2706lb (1230kg)

MAXIMUM SPEED
c202mph (325kph)

NUMBER MADE, DATES
349 built, 1995 – 1997

sold, not merely a pale imitation of it.

Although mechanically predictable, the rest of the car also set incredibly high engineering standards. There was a six-speed transmission in a magnesium casing, all-round coil spring independent suspension, with horizontally mounted, electronically-sensed Bilstein dampers which were operated via long F1-style 'push-rods' from the linkage. The cross-drilled and vented Brembo disc brakes were so large that they might even be confused for wheels instead. With centre-fix single-nut Speedline wheels – 8.5in. front rims and 13.5in. rear rims – and massive high-speed Goodyear Fiorano tyres, the F50 was a formidable car.

Anyone buying the F50 could look forward to utterly spine-chilling performance, and no-compromise motoring. Fitting snugly into lightly padded carbon fibre seats, the driver would find little carpet inside the cockpit, but a great deal of carbon fibre (even the gear lever knob). If motoring in dry conditions, the removable carbon fibre roof panel would be left at home (there was no provision for stowing it on board), and even Ferrari's sales staff admitted that the alternative soft-top ('the umbrella', as they whimsically called it) was useless above 30mph.

It is a measure of F1's pace of development that the F50 was already technically obsolete before it was previewed – by that time current cars were using 3-litre V10 power units – but Ferrari did not mind that. They had not revealed any technology before they were ready to do so, all the cars were pre-sold, and the limits of road-car motoring had been pushed back yet further. What on earth could they do for an encore ?

F550
MARANELLO

Front-engined instead of mid-engined ? A smooth, civilised, modern and spacious two-seater coupé, comfortable instead of a cramped, race-influenced two-seater cabin with the engine shrieking away behind your ears ? V12 instead of flat-12 ? Whatever next ?

Yet this is what happened in 1996, when Ferrari finally dropped the last of its flat-12 sports cars, and started a new line of V12-engined cars instead. The Boxer generation, introduced as long ago as 1973, was to be displaced by a new front-engined car. This was such an astonishing philosophical, design and marketing revolution that some cynics even wondered if the death of the 'Prancing Horse' badge, and Rosso red paintwork, would follow.

Although the new model, to be called 550 Maranello, was still a 'supercar' in anybody's language, it was an entirely new breed of Ferrari. Comfortable and refined where the earlier mid-engined models had been cramped, raucous and somehow slightly 'racier' – it acknowledged that current and future Ferrari owners would be the sort of independent rich, or successful businessmen who liked their colossal performance allied to peace and quiet, their handling and response more like that of other front-engined machinery – yet they wanted all this with tangible Ferrari character.

Under their new president, Luca de Montezemolo, Ferrari's policy was to provide new models which were more refined, far easier to live with, and vastly more practical than their predecessors. This was a deliberate shift in policy, and one which would become more apparent in the 2000s. Always, it seemed, there would be at least one indulgence in the range – like the recently-launched F50 – but future series-production Ferrari road cars would be much more gentlemanly than before. And so the 550 Maranello appeared, more Daytona than Boxer in style, and certainly more closely allied to the current 456GT model (which was a larger car) than to the F355 mid-engined model which was also in the range.

For 275GTB and Daytona lovers, this was the 1960s all over again, for the similarities in layout and in theme, if not in detail, were obvious. Way back in 1964, Ferrari had introduced the 275GTB, which had a novel layout, with a multi-tubular chassis frame, a V12 engine up front, and a rear-mounted combined transmission/final drive layout. All-independent suspension appeared for the first time on a true Ferrari road car. Here, now, in the 550 Maranello,

each of those elements, though in a different guise, was present once again. As always on such Ferraris, there was a multi-tube chassis frame, the engine had a 65-degree vee, the transmission had six forward speeds, and every element of the suspension (complete with the electronically sensed suspension dampers) was modern, and sophisticated.

Although the engine shared its vee angle with that of the F50 two-seater, there were no other similarities, for the 550 Maranello was an altogether larger and bulkier design, complete with a conventional four-valve-per cylinder twin-cam cylinder head layout. This brawny 484bhp/5.5-litre V12 also shared the same basic layout as the current 456GT 2+2 model, though it was much more powerful, and almost every other detail was new, not least the use of hydraulic tappets and Ferrari-patented variable-length inlet manifolds.

The six-speed transaxle too was shared with the 456GT, though with closer ratios, a higher top gear, and with an oil cooling radiator tucked away in the left rear wing. Ferrari's ASR traction control was standardised, but brave drivers could have more fun by switching this between 'normal' and 'sport' positions.

For once, though, the entire mechanical package, superlative or not, was often pushed into the background in favour of the style, and the general layout. Lovers of the now-discarded Boxer/Testarossa/512TR/512M had always

raved over the brutal charms of that mid-engined layout, complete with its wide rear track, and tricky handling. The new 550 was a complete contrast.

Naturally it was by Pininfarina, naturally the majority of cars would be painted in that unmistakable red, but in some ways this was rather a familiar-looking profile. The nose was low and wide, the flanks swooping, and the tail hump-backed with rather an abrupt cut-off, and there was even a touch of 275GTB in the general proportions. As with all the best V12-engined cars too, there were four exhaust pipes, protruding neatly from the rear bodywork.

Yet to the world-weary (are there such people, where Ferrari is concerned ?) this was not nearly as blood-stir-ring an offering as the mid-engined 12-cylinder cars had been. Maybe it was because there were not two, but four, headlamps under the glass cowls ? Maybe it was because the only side-positioned louvres were slanting outlets behind the front wheels ? And maybe it was because the *ensemble* looked, well, too integrated, too nice ?

No matter. This, above all, was a superlatively fast, civilised two-seater Ferrari, in which one could exceed any sensible road speed by a wide margin, while sitting back in comfort, in something approaching silence, and in the sure and certain knowledge that the chassis's limits were way above one's own. What was the point, after all, in carping about such a sophisticated and well-equipped machine,

The 550 Maranello was still a 'supercar' in anybody's language and an entirely new breed of Ferrari. Comfortable and refined, the superlative mechanical package was often pushed into the background in favour of the style and general layout.

when it could reach towards 200mph in favourable conditions, and in which it could outpace almost any other of the world's road cars ? And wasn't it better than the old-style mid-engined Ferraris ? According to the sales figures, undoubtedly yes, according to the performance figures, emphatically so, and in the customers' heart-of-hearts it was a clear step forward.

But, if this was to be the new theme at Ferrari, did it have to be be so silent ? And did have to be so, how can we put this, Teutonically efficient ? Whatever would Enzo Ferrari, the entrepreneur who famously held most of his retail customers in good-humoured contempt, have thought ?

F550 MARANELLO SPECIFICATION

ENGINE
65–deg V12

CAPACITY
5474cc

BORE X STROKE
88 × 75mm

COMPRESSION RATIO
10.8:1

POWER
484bhp

VALVE GEAR
Double overhead camshafts, four valves per cylinder

FUEL SYSTEM
Bosch Motronic engine management, and fuel injection

TRANSMISSION
Six-speed manual

FRONT SUSPENSION
Independent, by double wishbones, coil springs, electronic/telescopic dampers, anti-roll bar

REAR SUSPENSION
Independent, by double wish-bones, coil springs, electronic/telescopic dampers, anti-roll bar

BRAKES
All discs

WHEELS
Five–stud alloy

WEIGHT
3726lb (1690kg)

MAXIMUM SPEED
c199mph (320kph)

NUMBER MADE, DATES
Introduced 1996, still in production

360
MODENA

Here was a nightmare for a designer, even a resourceful Ferrari designer. One can imagine Luca de Montezemolo's vulpine grin, during a planning meeting, as he spat out these orders: 'We need a replacement for the F355. Yes, we know that the F355 car has sold very well. Yes, we know that everyone loves it. Yes, we know that the F355 was a huge step forward over the 348tb. Now you have to improve on this. For 1999, we want the next "small" Ferrari to be even better...'

Pandemonium! How on earth could the F355, complete with its standard-setting chassis, its amazing performance and service record, and its established appeal, be bettered ? But this was Ferrari, and although miracles always take a little time, there was surely scope to make a new car technologically more exciting, and its behaviour even better ? Read on...

It took time, but the result of Maranello's labours, the 360 Modena, was unveiled in March 1999 and disappointed no-one. For the first time in years, there was so much mechanical novelty under the skin, that the new car's style was almost ignored. Pininfarina, one feels, had rather expected this in any case, and they had produced a sinuous and workmanlike (though hardly ground-breaking) shape to cover the new mid-V8-engined chassis.

More shapely even than the F355 which was replaced, it featured so few air intakes that one wondered if they had been forgotten at the mock-up stage. Here was a car with no obvious full-width forward-facing scoop for the radiators, it sported the usual two side-mounted intakes for air to reach the engine bay, but no more. The engine lid was smooth and un-pierced, ahead of the windscreen there was an expanse of unbroken Ferrari paintwork, and this time the 550 Maranello-derived headlamps were under glass cowls rather than hiding behind pop-up panels. Tested exhaustively in Ferrari's own wind-tunnels, here was a car that developed four times the downforce of an F355 – which was more than any previous Ferrari road car.

Yet this was definitely a Ferrari, unmistakeably so. It wasn't merely the provenance of the style (to whom else did Pininfarina give so much attention ?), and it wasn't the fitting of discreet yellow 'Prancing Horse' badges to the nose, or to the centre of the five-spoke alloy wheels. It was, above all, the stance of the new car, the character which seemed to seep out of every contour, and that definite self-confidence that only such a Ferrari ever has.

This style hid a revolutionary new chassis in a package which was at once larger, lighter and more powerful than before. The secret was in the structure, largely made of aluminium, which might be more costly to produce in numbers, but gave the new car a real advantage. This car which was more spacious than its predecessors, and had the biggest yet – 3,586cc – version of the famous V8 engine, accelerated faster than ever, and could still return nearly 20 mpg in everyday (but exciting) motoring.

With acceleration from 0–60mph in a mere 4.2 seconds it could beat everyone else *and* wear out rear tyres at a prodigious rate – 0–100mph in 8.8 seconds was even faster than the F355 had ever achieved. The 36 Modena could endlessly produce such fierce acceleration, and yowl along autostradas at unheard-of average speeds. And do it with enormous style.

In its general layout, the 360 Modena owed much to the F355, but there were hundreds of changes in detail. The 90-degree V8, still with five-valves per cylinder, was behind the cabin, but ahead of the line of the rear wheels. Then the novelties began. For the first time, Ferrari offered six-speed longitudinally-positioned transmission, with the racing-type 'F1' fingetip gearchange option, as found on late-model F355s. Electronic drive-by-wire throttle control was standard too: who says that motor racing never reads across to road cars ?

The hybrid aluminium space-frame (no more steel tubes welded by artisans in small workshops close by), was clothed in an all-aluminium bodyshell, something not seen before on road cars, though found on the best of Ferrari's racing two seaters. Suspension wishbones in the all-independent installation were forged from aluminium instead of steel, the engine's cooling radiators were up front, tucked into the front corners, each of them fed by a blast

of cooling air from individual air intakes, and the power-assisted steering was lighter, quicker, and with a reduced lock-to-lock figure.

Other advances, too, showed in the detail, and in the statistics. The engine had a 2 mm longer stroke than ever before, just enough to add 90cc to the F355's capacity, and 20bhp to peak power (at 8,500rpm). The new car had a 5.9in/150mm longer wheelbase (which made the cabin more spacious), while the weight was 220lb/100kg lighter, yet technical director Amedeo Felisa claimed that the new-style light alloy structure was 44 per cent stiffer in torsional rigidity.

Nor had the suspension been forgotten, the handling had been trimmed by making the front tyres narrower and rear tyres fatter, while the Brembo disc brakes were larger and stopping distances had been reduced.

It is almost superfluous to mention that the 360 Modena delivered everything – in 'go', in 'stop', and in handling – that Ferrari claimed for it, and that it was not long before more than 2,000 cars were pouring out of Maranello's assembly halls in a year: many of these cars, incidentally, came with the 'F1' paddle-style gearchange operation.

The style of the 360 concealed a revolutionary new lightweight aluminium chassis which gave the new car a real advantage. The car was more spacious than its predecessors yet it accelerated faster than ever at 0–60mph in 4.2 seconds.

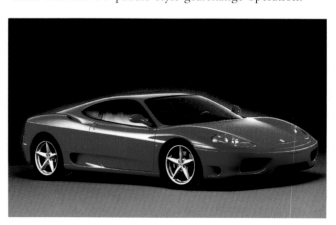

The performance, naturally was breathtaking, with all but first gear capable of pushing the 360 up to most open-road speed limits, and with even fourth gear (of six) good for 120mph. All this, together with armchair comfort in the driving seat – electric seat adjustment, and a steering wheel which could be moved up and down, or in and out – and a much revised driving position that finally allowed straight-leg motoring, meant that something like F40 performance was now available without effort.

What on earth could Ing. Felisa's team do to improve on this ?

F360 MODENA SPECIFICATION

ENGINE
90–deg V8

CAPACITY
3586cc

BORE X STROKE
85 × 79mm

COMPRESSION RATIO
11.0:1

POWER
400bhp

VALVE GEAR
Double overhead camshafts, five valves per cylinder

FUEL SYSTEM
Bosch Motronic engine management, and fuel injection

TRANSMISSION
Six-speed manual

FRONT SUSPENSION
Independent, by double wishbones, coil springs, electronic/telescopic dampers, anti-roll bar

REAR SUSPENSION
Independent, by double wish-bones, coil springs, electronic/telescopic dampers, anti-roll bar

BRAKES
All discs

WHEELS
Five–stud alloy

WEIGHT
3065lb (1390kg)

MAXIMUM SPEED
c183mph (295kph)

NUMBER MADE, DATES
Introduced 1999, still in production

INDEX

Additional photography credits:
Janus van Helfteren:
pp. 16–21, 22–63, 70–87, 94–111, 118–35
© *Salamander Books*.
Ian Kuah: *pp. 10–15, 64–9, 88–96, 112–17, 142–7, 154–9* © *Ian Kuah*.
Jim Forrest: *pp. 136–41, 149, 151, 152–3*
© *Salamander Books*.
Tim Andrew: *pp. 150*
© *Salamander Books*.
Pinifarina: *pp. 148*
Ferrari UK: *pp. 170–5*